Virginia Woolf

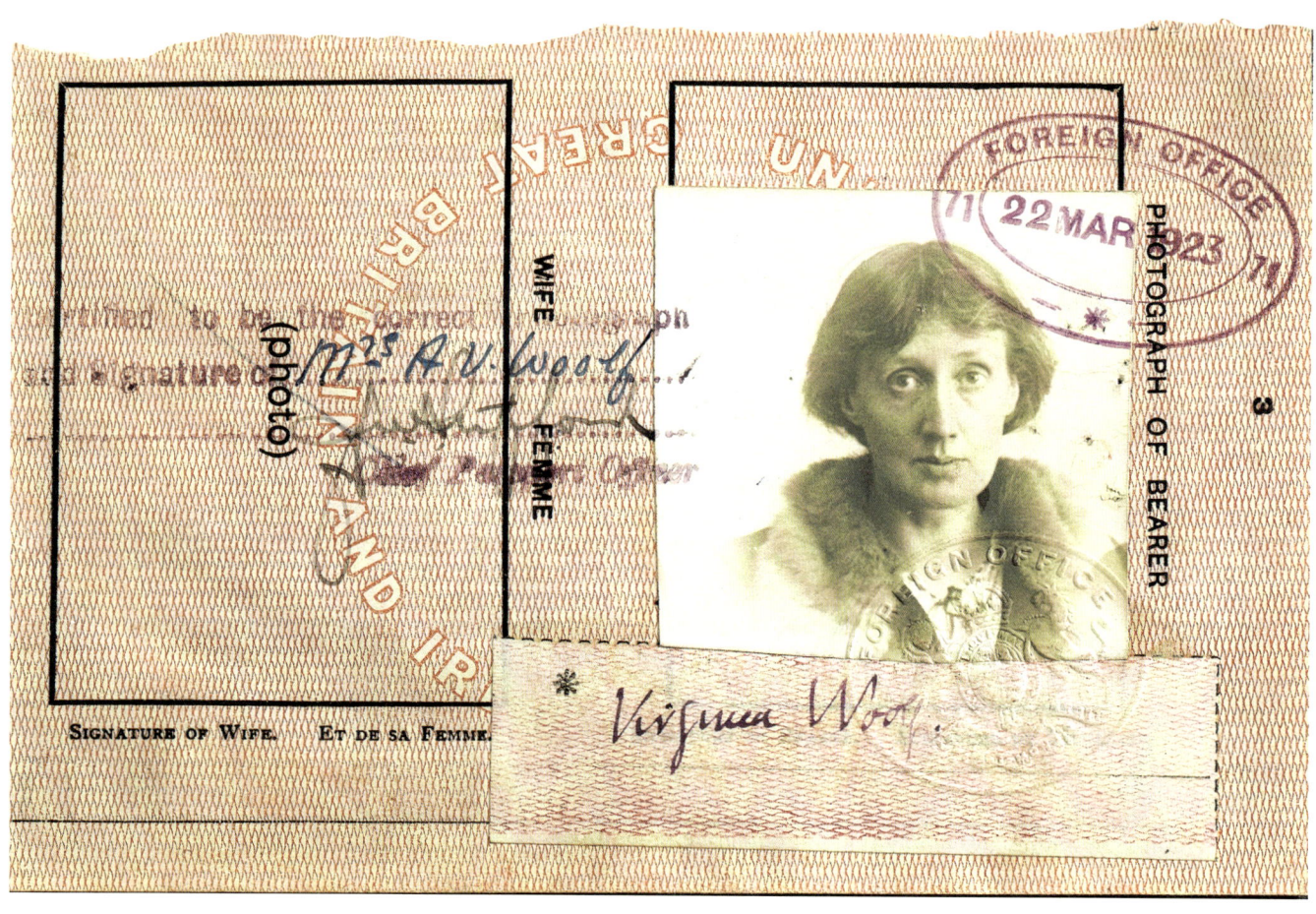

Virginia Woolf. Passport extract, signed.
Issued March 22, 1923 and valid through March 22, 1925.
Private collection

This Perpetual Fight

LOVE AND LOSS IN VIRGINIA WOOLF'S INTIMATE CIRCLE

by
SARAH FUNKE & WILLIAM BEEKMAN

with contributions by
Deirdre Bair, Rachel Cohen, Ruth Gruber, Mark Hussey,
Peter Stansky, Andrew Solomon, & Elizabeth Hartley Winthrop

THE GROLIER CLUB
New York City 2008

Published to accompany the exhibition at
The Grolier Club, New York City
September 16 through November 22, 2008

© 2008 Sarah Funke and William Beekman.

All rights reserved. The copyrights in the essays that appear at the start of each section are property of the respective authors.

Contents

INTRODUCTORY NOTE	7
I. GINIA STEPHEN: HER YOUTH AND FAMILY	11
The Old Man Elizabeth Hartley Winthrop	12
II. THE CAMBRIDGE MEN: VIRGINIA AND THE EMERGING PHILOSOPHY OF THE BLOOMSBURY GROUP	25
Conversazione Sarah Funke	26
III. BLOOMSBURY IN LOVE	37
Love in Bloomsbury William Beekman	38
IV. THE VISUAL ARTS IN BLOOMSBURY	51
The Arrival of Post-Impressionism in Bloomsbury Rachel Cohen	52
V. BOOKS AS OBJECTS: THE HOGARTH PRESS AND BEYOND	67
In Marriage, in Print, in Business Sarah Funke	68
VIA. HER LITERATURE: *Mrs. Dalloway*	83
"The Central Things" Sarah Funke	84
VIB. HER LITERATURE: *To the Lighthouse*	91
"Flown with Words" Sarah Funke	92
VII. HER ESSAYS AND THE GROUP'S FAME	95
The Chronicler and The Artist Deirdre Bair	96
VIII. HER FEMINISM: *Orlando*, *Three Guineas*, AND *A Room of One's Own*	105
The Fall of a Flower Mark Hussey	106
IX. THE NEXT GENERATION: VIRGINIA'S NEPHEWS JULIAN AND QUENTIN BELL	121
"Bubbling and boiling and frizzling": Virginia and the Next Generation Peter Stansky	122
X. THE GROUP AT AND AFTER HER DEATH	133
Ontology of a Suicide Andrew Solomon	134
Virginia Woolf: Her Courage to Write as a Woman Ruth Gruber	143
ABOUT THE AUTHORS	148
NOTES	149
BIBLIOGRAPHY	151

Introductory Note

The books, images, letters, and manuscript material detailed herein narrate Virginia Woolf's life and work through her relationships: with her parents and siblings; with her suitors, her friends, her lovers; and with her husband, Leonard Woolf. Virginia, with her sister Vanessa and brothers Thoby and Adrian, moved to Bloomsbury, a thitherto unfashionable part of London, upon the death of their father, Sir Leslie Stephen. They and formed the nucleus of what came to be known as the Bloomsbury Group: Leonard Woolf, Vanessa's husband Clive Bell and her lovers Duncan Grant and Roger Fry; Desmond and Molly MacCarthy; Lytton Strachey; John Maynard Keynes; E. M. Forster; and Saxon Sydney-Turner. This core group was, over time, enlarged and enlivened by T. S. Eliot, Dora Carrington, Vita Sackville-West, and others. These individuals, each of whom figured significantly in Virginia Woolf's life and work, included many who, like her, invented and popularized new paradigms in literature, the visual arts, economics and politics. They experimented publicly with ways of living that departed radically from the social mores of the previous generation. The Bloomsbury Group has been, virtually since the earliest meetings of their Memoir Club, their Thursday evening "At Homes," and their parties at Ottoline Morrell's, the subject of active gossip, admiration, scorn, envy, study, and debate.

We draw our title from Virginia's September 1934 diary entry, in which she reflects on the death of her good friend Roger Fry:

> I had a notion that I could describe the tremendous feeling at Roger's funeral: but of course I can't. I mean the universal feeling: how we all fought with our brains, loves and so on: and must be vanquished. A fear then came to me, of death. Of course I shall lie there too before that gate, and slide in, and it frightens me. But why? I mean, I felt the vainness of this perpetual fight, with our brains and loving each other, against the other things; if Roger could die.

The "universal feeling" was an express or implied theme in much of Virginia Woolf's fiction and non-fiction, and one that resonates with the story of her own life, from her childhood, through her loss of family, and of friends, and of security in two World Wars, to her struggles with mental illness and her eventual suicide. And yet Virginia was, by all accounts, a lively and engaging woman, full of warmth, humor, maternal feeling (for her sister's children, as she had none of her own), passion, and exultation. She had a prodigiously active career, and she stood at the center of a large group of notable, engaged figures, many of them public intellectuals at the forefront of their generation, who were connected to her (and to each other) by bonds of family, affinity, shared artistic and social enterprise and, above all, affection.

Virginia Woolf's novels are still widely read, but she also published influential literary criticism and feminist essays. Leonard Woolf was a political journalist, the editor of a number of prominent journals, and an intellectual founder of what would become the League of Nations. They came from different backgrounds (hers academic and genteel; his Jewish and professional), but they formed a lifelong bond in a marriage and in the formation of a press and publishing imprint. The Hogarth Press, which began as a hobby, solace, and diversion, grew into a flourishing business and (as the publisher of Freud in English, of Woolf herself, and of other authors such as T. S. Eliot, Katherine Mansfield, and Christopher Isherwood) an influential force in literary history.

Supporting characters include Virginia's parents, Leslie and Julia Stephen, so memorably portrayed as Mr. and Mrs. Ramsay in *To the Lighthouse*; her older sister, the artist Vanessa Bell, who married the art critic and bon vivant Clive Bell, bore two sons and a daughter (all adored by their aunt Virginia), and made her life in a farmhouse in Sussex that she decorated extravagantly with her lover and artistic collaborator, Duncan Grant; Grant's gay cousin, Lytton Strachey, the famously eccentric historian who proposed to Virginia and then, after she refused him, made his life with Dora Carrington, a beautiful young artist who married another man but dedicated her life to Lytton and committed suicide after his death; T. S. Eliot, whose early poetry was set by hand and first published in book form by the Woolfs; and the exotic, glamorous lesbian Vita Sackville-West, a best-selling author from a noble English family (and wife to Sir Harold Nicolson) who swept Virginia off her feet and then settled into the role of close friend (and Hogarth Press author).

This group, and their friends, produced mountains of books, hundreds of square feet of paintings, and reams of press. Our selection of material documents the mutual enrichment of their life and work, and the resonance of Virginia Woolf's greatest literary work (*Mrs. Dalloway, To the Lighthouse, Orlando, A Room of One's Own*, and more) with the story of her life and the lives of those who were dear to her.

We are pleased to make public, in some instances for the first time, material from a number of private collections. Items from William Beekman's collection of Virginia Woolf and Bloomsbury span her life and career, and include photographs, letters, association copies, artwork, and ephemera. From Barbara Dobkin's collection of feminist history we borrow a number of items from Virginia's adolescent library as well as material documenting her mature relationships. Additional material comes to us from Stuart Buice, and Sarah Funke; and through Abbot and Holder, James S. Jaffe, and Hans Kraus.

The Mortimer Rare Book Room at Smith College graciously provides many of the early images – drawn from Leslie Stephen's photo albums – as well as copiously annotated proof material and samples from Virginia's important correspondence with Lytton Strachey. Additional photographic material is derived from the Monk's House Albums, now housed in the Harvard Theatre Collection of The Houghton Library. The Henry W. and Albert A. Berg Collection of English and American Literature, Astor Lenox and Tilden Foundations, and The New York Public Library provides draft material from *Mrs. Dalloway*, manuscript notes for *To the*

Lighthouse, and Virginia's final diary entry. The Morgan Library & Museum loans an important essay manuscript. Permissions for the use of Woolf's letters and diaries are granted by the Society of Authors, as the literary representative of the Estate of Virginia Woolf.

This Perpetual Fight was designed by Barbara Suhr, mounted with the tireless assistance of Megan Smith, Exhibitions Coordinator of the Grolier Club, and installed with the assistance of members under the auspices of the Committee on Public Exhibitions. The accompanying catalogue was designed by Jerry Kelly and published under the auspices of the Grolier Club's Committee on Publications. The exhibit and catalogue would not have been possible without their help.

This Perpetual Fight is made possible in part through the generous support of Brandon Fradd, The Arthur F. and Alice E. Adams Charitable Foundation, and the Larson Charitable Foundation; of Nancy Newcomb and John Hargraves, Andrew Tobias, and Sue Ann Weinberg; and of several donors who prefer to remain anonymous. We are also grateful to our friends in the trade for their valuable contributions: Glenn Horowitz Bookseller; Bloomsbury Auctions, Christie's, Sotheby's, Swann Galleries; and Bonhams and PBA Galleries. Finally, we would like to thank our families, friends, and colleagues for their enthusiasm and expertise, especially Bunny Beekman, Mark Hussey, Karen Kukil, Abby Rosebrock, and Glenn Horowitz.

I. Ginia Stephen
Her youth and family

Virginia Stephen, ca. 1895
Private collection

The Old Man Elizabeth Hartley Winthrop

Leslie Stephen was 49 years old when Virginia Woolf was born in 1882, his third of four children by Julia Duckworth Stephen and his fifth child in total; it comes then as no surprise that he should figure in Woolf's writings almost exclusively as an "old man." As she writes of herself and her siblings in her memoirs, "We were not his children; we were his grandchildren. There should have been a generation between us to cushion the contact." But there was not, and so within the walls of Hyde Park Gate two different ages came up against each other: the socially rigid Victorian age as embodied by Leslie, and the more progressive, romantic Edwardian age as embodied by his children.

In many well-known photographs, Leslie Stephen appears as a long-bearded, slender man, his small eyes peering out from deep within folds of chiseled skin, his expression humorless and grave. It is a fitting image to complement the popular conception of Leslie as the brooding intellectual, obsessed with his work, obsessed with his reputation, obsessed with fame. Many readers think of Leslie as the eccentric, violent-tempered father, the "curious figure sitting often dead silent at the head of the family dinner table," the man who was said to have once "smashed a flower pot in a greenhouse," the writer "lying sunk in that deep rocking chair across [which] lay his writing board" or else "striding along, often shaking his head emphatically as he recited poetry" (as Woolf wrote in *A Sketch of the Past*). These traits are immortalized in the character of Mr. Ramsay in *To the Lighthouse*, whom Woolf closely modeled on her father; she titled one early scene "The Old Man (a character of L[eslie] S[tephen])." Like Leslie, Mr. Ramsay strides about in a world of his own, unabashedly reciting poetry. During the dinner scene, he "[sits] there scowling," and, just as Leslie is said to have smashed the flowerpot, Mr. Ramsay "finding an earwig in his milk at breakfast [sends] the whole thing flying through the air on to the terrace outside."

Both Mr. Ramsay and Leslie Stephen were preoccupied with genius and "childishly greedy for compliments," demanding reassurance particularly from their beloved wives. "It is when something happens to show me how little I have done," Leslie wrote in a letter to Julia on January 26, 1893, "that I feel as if I should like a little comfort and try to get it by complaining to you." Indeed, Woolf wrote in her memoirs that her mother was "too willing to sacrifice to [Leslie]," so that with her untimely death in 1895, she unwittingly left her children with the "legacy of his dependence." In the years that followed their mother's death, Virginia and her siblings lived under their father's heartbroken, gloomy tyranny. Devastated and insecure, he demanded constant sympathy and attention; he walked around the house quite literally groaning and beating his breast; he was given to abrupt and violent outbursts. In those years, Woolf has written, "the most imminent obstacle, the most oppressive stone laid upon our vitality and its struggle to live was of course father."

These years made a lasting impression on Woolf and certainly influenced her delineation of Mr. Ramsay's character, which is in part perhaps why the common perception of Leslie Stephen is that of a cantankerous, gruff, overgrown child largely indifferent to the feelings of his offspring. Quite the contrary is suggested, however, in letters Leslie wrote to his wife during Virginia's childhood. "Kiss my ragamice and Ginia. There will be no more of that breed," he wrote, fondly using Virginia's nickname; and: "Little Ginia is already an accomplished flirt. I said today that I must go down to my work. She nestled herself down on the sofa by me, squeezed her little self tightly up against me, and then gazed up with her bright eyes through her shock of hair and said, 'Don't go, papa.' She looked full of mischief all the time. I never saw such a little rogue." "My sweet little Ginia," he wrote in another letter. "I shall be glad to have her back." And: "My love to all my pets, specially my Ginia. I have been thinking of her all day."

Particularly in her later memoirs, "from [her] present distance in time," Woolf acknowledges her own deep love for her father. "Yes, certainly I felt his presence," she writes in *A Sketch of the Past*, "and had many a shock of acute pleasure when he fixed his very small, very blue eyes upon me and made me feel that we two were in league together." Recounting meeting her parents in the hall on their way to an evening out, she writes, "'I shall be glad when all this dining out is over, Jinny,' he said to me and I was flattered by his confidence; yet felt that he enjoyed it." And then, perhaps most telling of all about the nature of their relationship, Woolf recalls twisting a lock of hair in imitation of her father. "'Father does it,' I told my mother when she objected. 'Ah but you can't do everything father does,' she said."

But perhaps, in a way, Woolf wanted to. She recalls, as a child, reading books far beyond her understanding as quickly as she could in order to impress him, and swelling with pride at his compliments. She told him stories every night. Recognizing something of himself in her, Leslie wrote to Julia when Virginia was eleven: "Yesterday I discussed George III with her. She takes in a great deal, and will really be an author in time." Indeed, the similarities between father and daughter were striking. Both Stephen and Woolf were writers and great workaholics. Both were perfectionists; both were plagued by self-doubt. Both were afraid of beginning a piece of work. "The time it takes to screw up the courage and take the plunge is simply monstrous," Leslie wrote to Julia in October 1887. Likewise, Lily Briscoe, the character with whom Woolf identified as woman artist in *To the Lighthouse*, struggles with "where to make the first mark[.] One line placed on the canvas committed her to innumerable risks, to frequent and irrevocable decisions."

In *A Sketch of the Past*, Woolf acknowledges her "ambivalence" toward her father, the complex alternations of love and hate. She also attempts to write about him as someone separate from herself, "as he must have been, not to me, but to the world at large," recognizing the qualities of character that attracted people to him. She recalls,

Fred Maitland for instance told how they marched over the Cornish moors all day and Leslie was silent; "but I felt we had become friends"; and Lytton told me of some Strachey cousin who had watched my father as he sat by the fire swinging his foot, and every time his foot swung it knocked against a fire dog; and every time my father said "Damn"; but not another word. And the Strachey cousin was attracted.

This calls to mind a similar passage in *To the Lighthouse,* when William Bankes remembers a moment which gave an "odd illumination" into Mr. Ramsay's heart:

Bankes thought of Ramsay striding along a road by himself hung round with that solitude which seemed to be his natural air. But this was suddenly interrupted by a hen, straddling her wings out in protection of a covey of little chicks, upon which Ramsay, stopping, pointed his stick and said "Pretty – pretty."

Indeed, the ambivalence Woolf felt toward her father is apparent in her treatment of Mr. Ramsay. Despite all Mr. Ramsay's neediness and blustering and outrage, Woolf recognizes and acknowledges his humanity. At the end of the novel, Mr. Ramsay's daughter, Cam, regardless of the frustration and resentment she feels toward her father, comes to the conclusion that he is "not vain, not a tyrant [and that] she was safe, while he sat there," feelings that must have at times occurred to Virginia herself. Leslie Stephen died when he was 72; in a gesture of resurrection, the novel's final image of Mr. Ramsay is of the "Old Man" for whom the book was initially titled, "[springing], lightly like a young man, holding his parcel, on to the rock."

1. G. C. Beresford, *Leslie Stephen*

1902

Private collection

One of Leslie's photographic sittings was for G. C. Beresford in December 1902; the well-known Beresford portrait of Virginia was taken during this series of sittings as well. The style of the photograph, in its strong manipulation of light and dark, is eerily reminiscent of Julia Margaret Cameron. He is captured here several years after the death of his second wife, Julia, and just two years before his own passing. This is one of three prints of the photo signed by Leslie that devolved to his grandson, Quentin Bell.

2. Julia Margaret Cameron, *[Julia Prinsep Jackson] Stella*

(study of Mrs. Herbert Duckworth)

1867

Private collection, courtesy of Hans P. Kraus, Jr. Fine Photographs, New York

Julia Prinsep Jackson sat for her aunt and namesake Julia Margaret Cameron dozens of times throughout her life. Cameron took this portrait of Julia the year of her first marriage, to Herbert Duckworth. Just over 20, Julia was known for her beauty; a favorite model of Cameron, she also sat for Edward Burne-Jones and other pre-Raphaelite painters. Cameron titled the above portrait "Stella," comparing her niece with the "Stella" of the sixteenth-century sonnet series "Astrophel and Stella," likely by Philip Sidney, who writes of the allure of a star (Stella) to a mortal admirer:

> True, that true beautie virtue is indeed,
> Whereof this beautie can be but a shade,
> Which, elements with mortal mixture breed.
> True, that on earth we are but pilgrims made,
> And should in soule up to our countrey move:
> True, and yet true that I must Stella love.

Very much in love with her husband Herbert Duckworth, a wealthy barrister then in his mid-30s, Julia produced three children in four years: George, Stella, and Gerald, the last born six weeks after his father's sudden death from a burst abscess. Julia's mourning was extended and severe. As she began to recover, she read the essays of Leslie Stephen, among others. She became, like

Leslie, an agnostic, and devoted the balance of her too-brief adult life to a selfless schedule of good works, visiting the sick and needy. The seriousness of purpose she would adopt after Herbert's death is discernible in the photograph above. Cameron knew her niece intimately, and took her in during the earliest days of her mourning.

By 1875, however, Julia was ensconced, with her children, at 13 Hyde Park Gate – just doors down from the home into which she had helped Leslie Stephen move, with his sister-in-law, Anne Ritchie, and his daughter, Laura, in the wake of his own wife's unexpected death.

Leslie had married "Minny" (Harriet Marian) Thackeray in 1867, four years after the passing of her father, William Makepeace Thackeray. For a number of years they, too, had led an idyllic life. He doted on her; they traveled; they entertained. Together they had a single child, Laura, born in 1870 three months early and mentally disabled. In 1875 Minny once again went into labor prematurely; this time, neither mother nor infant survived. She died on her husband's 43rd birthday. (Laura lived till 1945, though by then an orphan and to all eyes at the Priory Hospital, Southgate, which she had called home for decades, an only child: Her Bloomsbury half-siblings took care of her expenses but nothing more.) Julia had been a friend to the Stephens, and once Leslie moved to Hyde Park Gate, after Minny's death, their intimacy increased. Leslie eventually overcame Julia's initial reluctance and the two were wed in 1878. Julia, still in her early 30s, gave Leslie – Herbert's contemporary – four children: Vanessa (b. 1879), Julian Thoby (b. 1880), Adeline Virginia (b. 1882), and Adrian (b. 1883).

Julia's death, like Minny's, was unexpected: she died in 1895 of influenza, not yet 50 and leaving behind her aging husband and eight children. Leslie, widowed for a second time, was inconsolable. The youngest child, Adrian, was twelve. Virginia Stephen was thirteen and her life and work would be graced and haunted by her mother's presence. Virginia had her first mental breakdown just after her mother died, and spent gallons of ink in subsequent years attempting to work out Julia's identity – traces are found in Rachel Vinrace's dead mother in her first novel, *The Voyage Out*; Mrs. Ramsay in *To the Lighthouse*; Eleanor Pargiter in *The Years*; and Julia Prinsep in a number of overtly autobiographical writings.

This portrait photo is one of many for which Julia sat for Cameron, who took to photography late in life. On her 50th birthday she received a camera from one of her daughters, who hoped to divert her from her loneliness. (Her husband had gone to Ceylon to tend his coffee plantation.) It was the beginning of a highly successful career in which Cameron obsessively posed and photographed friends, family, the famous and the obscure. Everyone who came within her sight was deployed into her lyrical portraits, from Tennyson, Carlyle, and Longfellow, to Ellen Terry, Darwin, and artist Holman Hunt, to servants, daughters of shoemakers, and town doctors. Virginia, always intrigued by her great-aunt – though as Cameron died in 1879 the two never met – owned many of her photographs, some of which she was able to retain throughout her many moves from city, to country, from house to house, and out of the path of the bombs raining on London during World War II. She also took to photography herself, enthusiastically shooting and developing her own photographs, many of which are preserved in the "Monk's House Albums" from which some of our illustrations are derived.

3. Leslie Stephen, "*American Humour*"
Manuscript, December 1865
Private collection

Original manuscript, fourteen pages, of Leslie Stephen's first piece for *Cornhill* magazine: an essay giving those in the colonies credit for no great literary, philosophical, or scientific achievement, but acknowledging the worth and character of a distinctly American sense of humor. Alas, his opinions were not shared by posterity, who found great merit, in fact, in the works of Emerson and Longfellow – "men of ability" who have not, however, "passed the second rank" – while the men he cites – Artemus Ward, Robert Henry Newell, Augustus Baldwin Longstreet, and others – are all but forgotten.

Leslie Stephen was one of the most esteemed men of letters of his day. Editor for over a decade of *Cornhill* magazine, a job he took over from his father-in-law William M. Thackeray, he left that post to assume the first editor's chair of the massive *Dictionary of National Biography* – from which he had to retire after eight years and 26 volumes because of the toll it was taking on his health and his marriage. In 1892 he succeeded Alfred, Lord Tennyson, as president of The London Library, and in 1902 he was knighted for his contributions to British cultural life. Throughout his career he was alternately an editor, promoter, and friend of Thomas Hardy, Henry James, George Meredith, James Russell Lowell – godfather to Virginia – and countless others, which perhaps explains his conservative evaluation of American masters of the literary craft.

Leslie began his *Cornhill* tenure as a regular contributor, and composed this heavily annotated manuscript in December 1865. It appeared in the January 1866 issue.

4. *The Duckworth and Stephen Children*
St. Ives, Cornwall, 1894
Mortimer Rare Book Room, Smith College

The Duckworth and Stephen children at St. Ives, the inspiration for the setting of *To the Lighthouse*. The Stephen family summered at Talland House, in St. Ives, Cornwall, from 1882 until Julia's untimely

death in 1895. It would later provide the inspiration for *To the Lighthouse*, for which Virginia's family served as models for some of the characters. Julia and nearly all her children – the four Stephens and the Duckworth boys (incorrectly captioned beneath the image by Leslie Stephen) – posed for the photograph above in 1892, a year before Julia's death. Stella Duckworth was likely behind the camera. (Also present are their friend Horatio Brown and their dog Shag.)

This photo is from an album Leslie kept of candid and posed photos taken between 1856 and 1894, printed in various sizes; most are captioned in his hand.

5. Vanessa, Thoby, and Virginia Stephen, *Hyde Park Gate News*

Manuscript. Volume I Number 51, Christmas Number
December 1891
The British Library

The cover of the Christmas 1891 issue of the Stephen children's family newsletter, prepared largely by Vanessa when Virginia was about ten years old. The tendencies of the Stephen children to imagine, put to paper, produce, and distribute ideas fanciful and critical almost from the cradle is seen in this family newsletter maintained in the 1880s and '90s through at least 69 issues (which survive at the British Library), nearly all in the hand of the eldest child, Vanessa. The cover for the Christmas issue of 1891 depicts "the celebrated author Mr. Leslie Stephen" with monocle and beard, sitting in a chair. News includes this about their mother: "The drawing-room of No 22 H.P.G. was crowded last Sunday with Christmas presents which the benignant Mrs. Leslie Stephen was about to bestow on her friends." And, of their grandmother: "Mrs. Jackson has as no doubt our readers know brought her canary with her to H.P.G. It far excels in singing Miss Vanessa Stephens bird. N.B. Miss Vanessa puts in her paper in whiteness of plumage instead of singing." In addition to "news," this and other issues include "correspondence" – questions and comments from their readers, the siblings – drawings, fiction, poetry, jokes and riddles, and more.

6. Anne Ritchie, *Records of Tennyson, Ruskin and Browning*

London: Macmillan and Co., 1892
Private collection

First edition of this history by the sister of Leslie Stephen's first wife, Minny Thackeray. Anne Thackeray Ritchie's family connections to the subjects of this book allowed her to create highly personal portraits of some of the most illustrious literary men of the period. This copy is a family gift, inscribed on the verso of the front endpaper by Leslie's second wife, Julia Stephen, to her first husband's sister, Minna Duckworth: *Minna Duckworth from Julia Stephen 1892.*

7. Virginia Stephen, "*The Sunset*"

In *The Life and Letters of Leslie Stephen* by Frederic William Maitland

    London: Duckworth & Co., 1906
    pp. 474-95
    Private collection

First edition of Woolf's first book appearance, and her first literary attempt to unravel her relationship with her father. She composed these "impressions of Sir Leslie Stephen by one of his daughters" following her second nervous breakdown and first suicide attempt, several months after her father's death. The number of copies printed is unknown, but was slight enough to justify a second printing the following year. It is likely that Leslie's stepson Gerald Duckworth underestimated the interest the volume would hold for readers outside the immediate circle of family and friends. In 1910, he reprinted it as part of their Crown Library series (Kirkpatrick B1a).

After Leslie's death in 1904, his friend Frederic Maitland – the husband of Virginia's first cousin, Florence Fisher – collaborated with Virginia on this biography, inviting her editorial assistance as well as this "note" on his life. In it, Virginia glosses over her father's less desirable characteristics, offering only occasional regrets; for example, "Greatly as I admired Stephen, I did not know how admirable he was until he was under sentence of death" (478). The pervasive tone is one of adoration; she concludes "that to have known Leslie Stephen is 'a part of our life's unalterable good.' 'And we may comfort ourselves, if comfort be needed, by the reflection that, though the memory may be transitory, the good done by a noble life and character may last beyond any horizon which can be realized by our imagination'"(495).

Life changed drastically in the Stephen household after the 1895 death of Julia. Virginia writes that "for some time after his wife's death, Stephen could hardly bear to let his children go out of his sight, and endeavored to preside in the schoolroom at great cost to his own peace of mind . Stephen would have liked to be both father and mother, and was grieved when he was told, as he had to be told, that his anxious and self-sacrificing solicitude was doing harm" (477). In response, he developed a sterner mask, a change that Virginia, perhaps naively, describes as beneficial: "All went better every year" (ibid.). In reality, Leslie distanced himself from his children when they needed him most. Virginia was in her early 20s when she wrote "The Sunset" for this volume; in a later memoir, published in *Moments of Being*, her tone is darker: "at the age of sixty-five he was a man in prison, isolated. He had so ignored, or disguised his own feelings that he had no idea of what he was; and no idea what other people were."[1]

"Woolf wrote and rewrote her father all her life. She was in love with him, she was furious with him, she was like him, she never stopped arguing with him,"[2] writes Hermione Lee, tracing his appearances throughout Virginia's work from "The Sunset," through her memoirs and diaries, and into her fiction. For the rest of her life Virginia struggled with his ghost, simultaneously reflecting his work habits and abilities, while consciously removing herself from his sphere of influence, rebelling not just against him, but against the writing of his generation.

8. Vanessa Stephen, *Julia, Leslie, and Virginia Stephen*

Talland House, St. Ives, Cornwall
1893

Mortimer Rare Book Room, Smith College

Julian and Leslie reading, at Talland House, with young Virginia – here, about 11 years old – in the background. Virginia took to reading from an early age. At 15 she was granted by her father unprecedented access to his library, and took part in what was surely the most exclusive book club in England at that time: in addition to reading whatever she chose from his shelves on her own, she took in specific texts Leslie assigned for discussion.

Books were, in every way, the currency of their context, by the children's reading them, critiquing them, writing about them, eventually in writing books themselves, and in giving and receiving them on loan or as gifts. Below are a number of volumes that changed hands among the Stephen clan, as well as precious books from Virginia's own library.

9. John Keats, *The Poetical Works*

Edited with an introduction and textual notes by H. Buxton Forman
Oxford: Oxford University Press, 1906

Private collection

A gift copy, inscribed on the front endpaper to Virginia by Violet Dickinson: *A.V.S. from V.D. 1906*. Virginia became an intimate friend of Violet in 1902, and in 1903 at times wrote to her every other day, addressing her as "My Beloved Woman" and confiding the details of her father's illness and her own physical and emotional state. By 1936, Dickinson had accumulated 350 letters from Woolf, most dating from this early period. In May 1903 Virginia wrote: "Your letters come like balm on the heart. I really think I must do what I never have done – try to keep them. I've never kept a single letter all my life – but this romantic friendship ought to be preserved." In July she wrote of the "astonishing depths – hot volcano depths" Dickinson had stirred in her. After her father's death in 1904, Woolf convalesced from a nervous breakdown at Dickinson's home, where she made her first suicide attempt – through defenestration. In 1906 they traveled, with Vanessa, to Greece, where they met up with the Stephen brothers Adrian and Thoby. Both Thoby and Violet contracted typhoid on the journey, but only Violet recovered. The two continued to correspond, and Virginia presented Violet, in 1907, with a typescript mock biography of her, prepared in violet ink – Virginia's signature ink throughout her career, "Waterman's fountain pen ink. Cheap, violet, indelible"[3] – and specially bound in violet leather.

With Vanessa's marriage to Clive Bell in 1907, Virginia's move to Brunswick Square in 1911, and her 1912 marriage to Leonard, Virginia redirected her attentions to life in Bloomsbury, and her exchanges with Dickinson slowed, but never stopped. Though the two never revisited the intensity of those first years, they kept in touch irregularly throughout their lives. Woolf wrote in her diary of a May 1919 visit: "She hasn't changed a hair for 20 years, which must be the length of our friendship. We take things up precisely as we left them; a year's gap makes no difference; we have had our intimacy; something or other has fused; & never hardens again." Dickinson is mentioned in the ironic preface to *Orlando* among the friends who helped Woolf "in ways too various to specify."

Keatsian allusions, references, and themes are evident throughout Woolf's oeuvre, but they are especially pronounced in the earlier works, notably *The Voyage Out, Jacob's Room, Mrs. Dalloway* and *A Room of One's Own*. Mark Hussey, who has traced these references and influences, further notes that Keats and other Romantic poets provided a spiritual foundation in her creative processes.

10. Thomas Hardy, *The Mayor of Casterbridge*
London: Macmillan, 1908

A Pair of Blue Eyes
London: Macmillan, 1910

A Laodicean
London: Macmillan, 1912
Private collections

Virginia's copies of three volumes of the Wessex Novels series of Thomas Hardy's Works. Each signed on the front endpaper, *V. Stephen*.

On the train to meet Hardy for the first and only time, on July 23, 1926, Virginia read through *The Mayor of Casterbridge*. She had already anxiously written to Vita Sackville-West: "I'm dashing off, you'll be amused to hear, on my chronic visit to Hardy . I shall only stay one day and drink one cup of tea, and be so damned nervous I shall spill it on the floor, and what shall I say? Nothing, but arid nonsense. Yet I feel this is a great occasion. Here am I approaching the immortal fount, touching the sacred hand ."[4] During the visit Hardy recalled her father's courageous publication of *Far from the Madding Crowd*; Virginia immortalized his comment in her diary: "We stood shoulder to shoulder against the British public about certain matters dealt with in that novel." Leslie had promoted Hardy's early fiction in *Cornhill*, but in 1877 even he deemed *The Return of the Native* too provocative for his conservative magazine. Hardy inscribed a copy of *Life's Little Ironies* for Virginia to take away as a souvenir of her visit to Max Gate.

One week after Hardy's death on January 11, 1928, Virginia anonymously published the obituary on which she had been working, off and on, since 1919: "Thomas Hardy's Novels" appeared in the *TLS* on January 19, 1928, and was later revised for *The Common Reader: Second Series* (1932) and later publications. In 1936, while struggling with *The Years*, she read Hardy's *The Trumpet Major*, and expressed a revised opinion: "He had genius & no talent." In her obituary she takes pains to illustrate the difference between the two, concluding that despite the many "imperfections" in many of his novels, on the whole "The effect is commanding and satisfactory":

> We have been freed from the cramp and pettiness imposed by life. Our imaginations have been stretched and heightened; our humour has been made to laugh out; we have drunk deep of the beauty of the earth. Also we have been made to enter the shade of a sorrowful and brooding spirit which, even in its saddest mood, bore itself with a grave uprightness and never, even when most moved to anger, lost its deep compassion for the sufferings of men and women. Thus it is no mere transcript of life at a certain time and place that Hardy has given us. It is a vision of the world and of man's lot as they revealed themselves to a powerful imagination, a profound and poetic genius, a gentle and humane soul.

11. Walter M. Gallichan, *The Story of Seville*

With three chapters on the artists of Seville by C. Gasquoine Hartley. Illustrated by Elizabeth Hartley
London: Dent, 1903
Private collection

First edition of this brief history of Seville, told through its streets, its architecture, and its artists. From young Virginia's library with an early signature on the front endpaper: *Virginia Stephen, March: 1905*.

12. John and Margaret Paston and family, *The Paston Letters 1422-1509 A.D.*

A reprint of the edition of 1872-5, which contained upwards of five hundred letters, etc., till then unpublished, to which are now added others in a supplement after the introduction. Edited by James Gairdner
Westminster: Constable, 1901
Private collection

New edition, edited and expanded, with nearly one thousand letters and related documents arranged chronologically in sections marked by the reigns of kings as follows: Henry VI, Edward IV, Henry VI restored, Edward IV, and Henry VII. Signed on the front endpaper of volume three: *Virginia Stephen 1905*.

In "The Pastons and Chaucer," an essay that appeared in *The Common Reader* in 1925, Virginia wrote on the lives of John Paston, his wife Margaret, and their children and grandchildren, as revealed by these four volumes of letters that document the intimate and public lives of three generations during the fifteenth century. Though Mark Hussey notes that Virginia read these letters, along with the Arber edition of the letters (1872-1874), and *The Pastons and Their England: Studies in an Age of Transition* by H. S. Bennett (Cambridge University Press, 1922) from late 1921 through 1922, the 1905 date that accompanies her signature in this set indicates that she was introduced to the Pastons substantially earlier. Indeed, almost upon receipt of them she planned an essay: she wrote to Violet Dickinson at the end of August 1905, "I am writing 2 large works; one upon the letters of the Paston family; the other upon the nature and characteristics of the county of Cornwall; I want to learn how to write descriptions without adjectives. Both works show remarkable promise – because they are still unwritten."

Despite this early enthusiasm, she did not revisit the idea until the fall of 1921: in her diary she recorded the desire to conjure energy sufficient to tackle the project, then tentatively entitled "Reading."[5] One evening in January 1922 she noted that her reading of the Pastons had commenced, but two days later she was struck with influenza. That August she took a break from writing *Mrs. Dalloway* and focused on "Reading": "I wrote 4 thousand words of Reading in record time, 10 days; but then it was merely a quick sketch of Pastons, supplied by books. Now I break off, according to my quick change theory, to write Mrs. D . then I do Chaucer; & finish the first chapter early in September."[6] By October 1922, *Mrs. Dalloway* and the Chaucer portion of the Paston essay were complete, and she declared that much fruit had been borne by reading Chaucer and the Pastons simultaneously, "So evidently my plan of the two books running side by side is practicable, & certainly I enjoy my reading with a purpose."[7]

A serious historical document of life during the reigns of Henry VI, Edward IV, and Richard III, these letters reveal the inner workings of a family within the context of its society, as well as their individual household roles and relationships. Of special note here is Virginia's assessment of the letters of Mrs. Margaret Paston: "The long, long letters which she wrote so laboriously in her clear cramped hand to her husband, who was (as usual) away, make no mention of herself."

Virginia discusses the place of girls and women at some length: which transgressions merited a beating by a mother or brother, which merely called for the girl to be "turned out of the house," and which permitted interference to be run between a daughter and an offended family member. She ties the essay together with the failure of John Paston's son to secure for him a tombstone, and the vagaries of his life and personality that led to this failure, including his voracious reading, uncharacteristic for one of his set and time.

13. Virginia Woolf, *The Voyage Out*
London: Duckworth & Co., 1915
Private collection

First edition of Woolf's first novel, published by her half-brother, Gerald Duckworth; 2,000 copies were printed (Kirkpatrick A1a).

This copy is from the library of her early mentor Janet Case, signed by her on the front endpaper in the month of publication: *Janet Case / March 25, 1915*. Case, a classicist, feminist, and pacifist, became Virginia's Greek tutor in 1902. Their friendship developed gradually, with Virginia's youthful devotion and adolescent infatuation cooling at Janet's articulation of clashing views. In 1918, when the animated discussions they had over contemporary literature led Virginia to suspect criticism not just of her chosen profession, but specifically of *The Voyage Out*, she realized that "such encounters, are bound to happen every month of one's life":

> It's the curse of a writer's life to want praise so much, & be so cast down by blame, or indifference. The only sensible course is to remember that writing is after all what one does best; that any other work would seem to me a waste of life; that on the whole I get infinite pleasure from it; that I make one hundred pounds a year; & that some people like what I write.[8]

Her relationship with Case and with her sister, Euphemia ("Emphie"), waned as Janet's criticism grew more pointed, and as she and Emphie moved away for economic reasons in 1919. In the spring of 1937, Woolf discovered Janet was dying of cancer, and her emotions re-warmed. She closed one of the last letters she wrote to Janet with her esteem for both: "My love to Emphie, whom I think one of the nicest women I ever met. And to Janet too" (May 26, 1937). Woolf penned Janet's obituary for the *Times*, which appeared on July 22, 1937, a week after her death.

In *The Voyage Out*, Virginia tackles the predicament of young women of her age and class regarding education, marriage, and profession. Throughout the novel's composition, publication, and reception, she was racked with anxiety. She began it as *Melymbrosia* in 1908, basing it on her voyage from Liverpool to Oporto by sea a few years before. After four thorough revisions, during which she removed as much autobiographical material as possible, she offered it in 1913 as *The Voyage Out* to her half-brother, Gerald Duckworth, for his imprint, despite tensions existing between them (Woolf had earlier rebuffed his romantic advances, which had constituted a significant event in *Melymbrosia*). Even after publication, almost two years to the day after she submitted the manuscript – mental instability occasioned some delay – she was dissatisfied, agreeing with Lytton Strachey that it "failed in its overall conception." (Lytton had, however, also written her that he "adored" the book, Tolstoyian in scope and with characters of whom Shakespeare wouldn't have been ashamed: "I read it with breathless pleasure, the minute it came out . I don't think I ever enjoyed the reading of a book so much." The greatest compliment of all? "Oh, it's very, very unvictorian!"[9])

By the end of the decade, Virginia's rereading elicited a combination of embarrassment, wistful pride, and concern about the place of women in the world of letters. She revised it again further for Doubleday, Doran's American edition in 1920.

II. The Cambridge Men
Virginia and the Emerging Philosophy of the Bloomsbury Group

Leonard Woolf with G. E. Moore. Asheham, June 1914
Reprinted by permission of the Harvard Theatre Collection, The Houghton Library

Conversazione Sarah Funke

Julian Thoby Prinsep Stephen – "Thoby" to his family and friends – was by all accounts the most sociable, charismatic, and robust of the Stephen children. In 1905, after the death of their father, he began hosting Thursday evening "At Homes" as a way to maintain connections with his college friends, and to share them – and their ideas and conversation – with his sisters Vanessa and Virginia. Thus the Bloomsbury Group, named for the part of London to which Thoby and his sisters had moved after their father's death, was born.

Thoby entered Trinity College of Cambridge University in 1899, and formed close relationships with Lytton Strachey, Leonard Woolf, and Clive Bell. In 1902 Leonard and Lytton were inducted, with their classmate Saxon Sydney-Turner, into the Cambridge Conversazione Society – a secret society compelling lifelong affiliation, founded in 1820 to unite the most intellectually provocative students. E. M. Forster, Desmond MacCarthy, and Roger Fry were already Apostles – so called for the number of undergraduate members at any one time. John Maynard Keynes would be elected the following year, and James Strachey, still later. (Clive and Thoby were not tapped for membership.)

The Society took on a mildly cult-like aspect under the influence of philosopher and Cambridge don G. E. Moore, whose shaping power over the incipient Bloomsbury Group permeates their memoirs, diaries, and letters. In *My Early Beliefs*, a foundational Bloomsbury document, Maynard describes Moore's *Principia Ethica* as the bible of his generation's new religion:

> I went up to Cambridge at Michaelmas 1902, and Moore's Principia Ethica came out at the end of my first year. I have never heard of the present generation having read it. But, of course, its effect on us, and the talk which preceded and followed it, dominated, and perhaps still dominates, everything else. We were at an age when our beliefs influenced our behaviour, a characteristic of the young which it is easy for the middle-aged to forget, and the habits of feeling formed then still persist in a recognisable degree. The influence was not only overwhelming it was exciting, exhilarating, the beginning of a renaissance, the opening of a new heaven on a new earth, we were the forerunners of a new dispensation, we were not afraid of anything. Now what we got from Moore was by no means entirely what he offered us. We accepted Moore's religion, so to speak, and discarded his morals.[10]

Moore's ideas infiltrated his Cambridge friends and protégés through weekly Apostle meetings, annual reading parties, and irregular discussions. Moore biographer Darlei Dall'Agnol writes of one thread that particularly appealed to the Bloomsbury Group: friendship. Moore writes, "we may admit that the appreciation of a person's attitude towards other persons, or, to take one instance, the love of love, is far the most valuable good we know, and far more than the mere love of beauty, yet we can only admit this if the first be understood to *include* the latter, in various degrees of directness." Of course, as Dall'Agnol points out, "*Principia Ethica* does not claim that moral duties are subservient to art" – and this was the source of much debate among the young men of Cambridge.[11]

The women of Cambridge, so to speak – Vanessa and Virginia – entered the circle through Thoby, and soon were its hostesses. In examining the formation of the Bloomsbury Group, Saxon Sydney-Turner wrote to Virginia in 1919 that some members came already bonded – as family; others fell in easily – through Thoby, Lytton became one of Virginia's closest friends; Leonard, her husband; Clive, her brother-in-law; and for some it took more time. "Perhaps also it's easier between man and man," he wrote. "I remember that at one time I thought you rather difficult."[12] Virginia ultimately encountered Moore, too, the man and his works, through Thoby and his friends. According to Moore biographer Paul Levy, the influential philosopher was "in fact on more intimate terms [with Virginia] than one would guess from the paucity of the mentions of each in the other's diaries."[13]

Virginia first met Moore in 1916, and she readily accepted his friendship. "He is quite easy, and much more human than his followers; but one can see how they've copied him, but he has much more vigour than they have. Perhaps they no longer exist though," she wrote Vanessa.[14] She described the visit to Saxon:

> He, too, came with a box like lead, and it was full of music books, which he meant to sing to us, but we had no piano, so he sang without one – some very nice old German and English songs. Do you know one about the 'foggy foggy dew', and another about 'lost in the Lowland seas'? He is a very great man, I think, so solid and direct: and not the least hard to talk to. He knows all the wild flowers and butterflies. He spent his time writing a review, and when he went he had scratched it all out and begun a new one.[15]

She remained skeptical, however, of the esteem in which her intimates held his theories. Her reading while composing *The Voyage Out* included *Principia Ethica*. She wrote Clive that she had been "climbing Moore like some industrious insect, who is determined to build a nest on the top of a Cathedral spire. One sentence, a string of 'desires' makes my head spin with the infinite meaning of words unadorned; otherwise I have gone happily."[16] This experience made its way, more lightly, into her novel: Hussey notes, "Richard Dalloway picks up the book that Helen Ambrose is reading and reads aloud a passage from chapter 1, section 17 of *Principia Ethica*, remarking that it is 'jolly to think that's going on still.'" In her diary as late as June 17, 1918, Virginia notes, "We discussed the moral eminence of Moore, comparable to that of Christ or Socrates, so R[ay Strachey]. & L[eonard Woolf]. held. They challenged me to match him in that respect by any of my friends. I claimed for Nessa, Duncan, Lytton, & Desmond something different but of equal value." Decades later, in 1940, she referred to Moore's work, perhaps with a wink, as "the book that made us all so wise and good."[17]

14. G. E. Moore, *Principia Ethica*
Cambridge: Cambridge University Press, 1903
Private collection

First edition of Moore's first book: his masterwork, and a wellspring of Bloomsbury thought. Though he regularly published essays and articles, none of his later books – which include *Ethics* (1912), *Philosophical Studies* (1922), and *Some Main Problems of Philosophy* (1953) – ever achieved the popular or cult status of *Principia Ethica*.

A presentation copy, inscribed on the half-title to his sister Henrietta: *To Hettie with best love from George. Christmas, 1903*. Of his seven brothers and sisters, Hettie, one year his senior, and Tom, were the closest to George throughout his life.

15. Cambridge Conversazione, *Invitation to Apostles Dinner*
Ca.1914
Private collection

This invitation reads,

> The Cambridge Conversazione will dine (7 for 7:15) at The Connaught Rooms, Great Queen Street, On June 26th. R.S.V.P. Desmond MacCarthy, 25. Wellington Square, Chelsea, S.W.

Signed in print by Desmond MacCarthy, it also includes his autograph note: "Please come. D." MacCarthy was initiated into the Apostles in 1896 – nearly a decade after Roger Fry (elected 1887) but several years before Forster (1901), Keynes (1903), Leonard, Lytton, and Saxon (1902-03), and James Strachey (1906). He devoted his career to writing and editing cultural criticism – including much literary commentary under the name "Affable Hawk," and including much on the work of Virginia and her friends. Though no year is given on this invitation, the London address dates it to, mostly likely, his post-graduate years, and we assume it was sent to Leonard: the current owner purchased it at an auction for the benefit of the Charleston Trust, to which it was donated by Quentin Bell's daughter, Virginia.

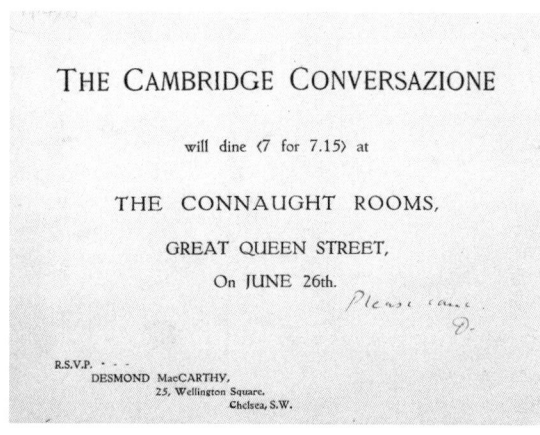

16. (Cambridge Men) *Euphrosyne*
A collection of verse

Published and sold by Elijah Johnson, 30 Trinity Street, Cambridge
London agents: Messrs. A. & F. Denny, 147 Strand
(August) 1905
Private collection

This collection of poems by Clive, Lytton, Leonard, Thoby, Saxon, and their Cambridge friend Walter Lamb was anonymously published, and any attempt to research details of authorship is thwarted by the vague prefatory note: "A few of the following Poems have already appeared in Magazines, to the Editors of which we make all acknowledgements."

Virginia, though, outed the writers in a 750-or-so-word essay she drafted but never completed, dated May 21, 1906. In it, she mocks their conceit and derides their talent, devoting little space to textual analysis of their "few songs & sonnets" from their "astoundingly brilliant & immoral productions" composed to read to each other. She devotes even more ink to lampooning the gender-bias of the education system:

> Among all the advantages of that sex which is soon, we read, to have no [dis]advantages, there is much to be said surely for that respectable custom which allows the daughter to educate herself at home, while the son is educated by others abroad.
> At least I am fain to think that system beneficial which preserves her from the omniscience, the early satiety, the melancholy self satisfaction which a training at either of our great universities produces in her brothers.

The authors of this volume, she writes, "entered the College, young & ardent & conceited;

> pleased with themselves, but so well pleased with the world that their vanity might be forgiven them. They return not less impressed with their own abilities indeed, but that is the last illusion that is left to them ... they say, that success is failure & they despise success." It is perhaps because they fear to fall a victim to its snares that they are generally silent, & express for the most part a serene & universal ignorance; which does not disqualify them however to pronounce the opinions of others absurd.

They admire only the work of the most obscure of writers (and "if the public show signs of appreciating the same things [they dexterously transfer their praise to some more obscure head]") and of each other – that is, the works they've yet to write. As for the present volume, they "sang of Love & Death & Cats, & Duchesses, as other poets have sung before, & may, unless the race is extinct, sing yet again . But when taxed with their melancholy the poets confessed that such sadness had never been known, & marked the last & lowest tide of decadence."[18]

Virginia never quite let go of this event as a source of gentle needling of her brothers, her husband and friends: she names for this collection the ship in her first novel, *The Voyage Out*, and also a character in *Orlando*.

17. Virginia Woolf, *The Years*

London: The Hogarth Press, 1937
Private collection

First edition, in the dust-jacket designed by Vanessa; one of two jacket designs Vanessa signed with her full name (the other is *Between the Acts*). Over 18,000 copies printed (Kirkpatrick A22, Woolmer 423). A presentation copy, inscribed on the front endpaper: *Saxon from Virginia.*

Saxon Sydney-Turner was known as something of a literary savant at Cambridge, and his presence at Thoby's inaugural "Thursday Evening" in 1905 marked him as one of the first members of the Bloomsbury Group. Virginia included him in her farcical preface to *Orlando,* praising his "wide and peculiar erudition." "According to Thoby," through whom the Stephen sisters heard vivid portraits of his Cambridge friends prior to meeting, "Sydney-Turner was an absolute prodigy of learning," Virginia wrote in her essay "Old Bloomsbury," delivered at the Memoir Club and published in *Moments of Being*:

> He had the whole of Greek literature by heart. There was practically nothing in any language that was any good that he had not read. He was very silent and thin and odd. He never came out by day. But late at night if he saw one's lamp burning he would come and tap at the window like a moth. At about three in the morning he would begin to talk. His talk was then of astonishing brilliance. When later I complained to Thoby that I had met Turner and had not found him brilliant Thoby severely supposed that by brilliance I meant wit; he on the contrary meant truth. Sydney-Turner was the most brilliant talker he knew because he always spoke the truth.[19]

18. C. N. S. Woolf, *Poems*

London: The Hogarth Press, 1918
Private collection

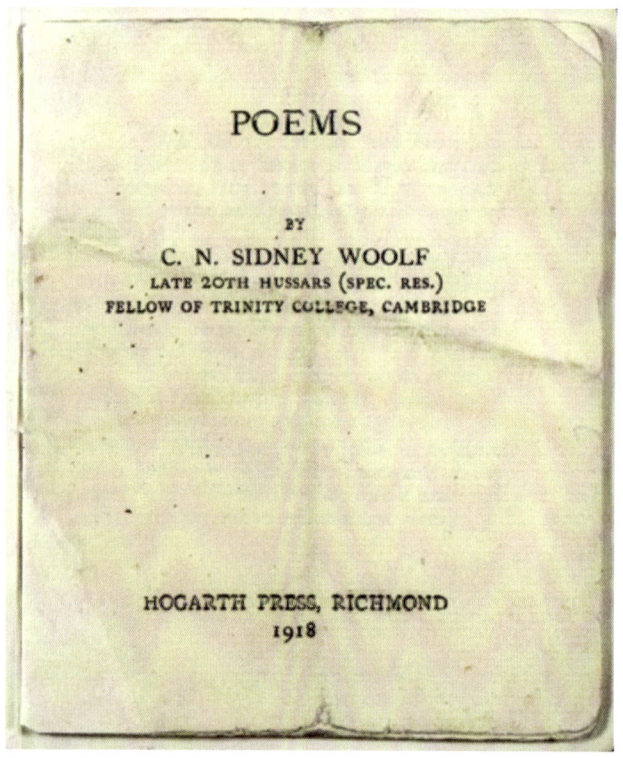

First edition of this slender, humbly constructed volume of poetry by Leonard's younger brother Cecil. Virginia and Leonard halted work on Katherine Mansfield's *Prelude* to prepare, with Leonard's brother Philip, this memorial to Cecil, killed in combat the previous year at the Battle of Cambrai in France; number of copies printed unknown, but possibly only nine copies in existence – likely more than Virginia had hoped would survive. She wrote in her diary of these poems: "They're not good; they show the Woolf tendency to denunciation without the vigour of my particular Woolf."[20] Philip set some of the type; he "had been wounded by the same shell that killed Cecil."[21] (Woolmer 3) Leonard was the fourth of ten children (though the second died in infancy). Cecil was seven years his junior and Philip, nine. Though two of Leonard's brothers were married twice, after Philip's wife committed suicide Philip chose to live with his sister Bella. After her death, he, too, took his own life.

19. Adrian Stephen, *The Dreadnought Hoax*

London: The Hogarth Press, 1936
Private collection

First edition of this brief account written by Virginia's younger brother Adrian, who organized the famous prank with his Cambridge friend, Horace Cole. The photograph on the cover depicts the "Emperor of Abyssinia" and his entourage, including a dark-skinned, bearded "fellow" on the far left, Miss Virginia Stephen. Though over 2500 copies were printed, more than half were later pulped (Woolmer 396).

Dust jacket photo, left to right: *Virginia, Guy Ridley, Adrian, Anthony Buxton, Duncan, Horace de Vere Cole*

The youngest and most introverted Stephen sibling, Adrian Leslie Stephen is immortalized in *To the Lighthouse* as the child who does not get to join his siblings on the title excursion. Though he attended Cambridge, as had Thoby, he chose for himself a different path, acquiring a reputation as a hoaxster. The *Dreadnought* hoax of 1910 was the most elaborate scheme he hatched: Adrian, Virginia, Duncan Grant, and a few friends disguised themselves in robes and make-up to pay a state visit to a British battleship, as the Emperor of Abyssinia and his court. The frontispiece depicts six of them in costume: "The Emperor of Abyssinia" and His Suite includes Adrian, Virginia, Duncan, Anthony Buxton, Guy Ridley, and Horace Cole; "The Sultan of Zanzibar" and His Suite shows Adrian and Cole with Bowen Colthurst, Leland Buxton, and "Dummer" Howard; the final image is of the HMS *Dreadnought*.

After Thoby's early death and Vanessa's marriage, Adrian and Virginia lived together and continued the Thursday evening "At Homes" begun by Thoby, which were the origin of the Bloomsbury Group. But after Virginia's marriage, Adrian drifted to the fringes of Bloomsbury life.

20. Virginia Woolf, *Autograph letter signed to Sydney Waterlow*

December 9, 1911
Private collection

Virginia writes generously to a married friend whose proposal – to leave his wife and marry her – she had rejected only weeks before. She wants to clarify her stance, and quash any lingering hope he might be harboring: "I don't think I shall ever feel for you what I must feel for the man I marry . I feel you have it in your power to stop thinking of me as the person you want to marry. It would be unpardonable of me if I did not do everything to save you from what must – as far as I can tell – be a great waste. I hope we shall go on being good friends anyhow."

Sydney Waterlow was an early friend of Clive Bell and a regular participant in Bloomsbury Group events until his diplomatic activities removed him from their sphere in the mid-1920s. Though Waterlow was responsible for implementing some of Leonard's theories of government at the Paris Peace Conference, he appeared in subsequent years in Virginia's letters and diaries as an object of somewhat bitter mirth. In 1912, for example, when Waterlow moved to Richmond with his new wife, Virginia wrote in her diary: "I don't know why exactly, but no one I've ever met seems to me more palpably second rate and now the poor creature resigns himself to it." In 1921 she tried to explain to Waterlow that her feelings toward him were, in fact, mixed, though the negative impressions seemed more likely to rise to the surface. In the summer of 1922, having spied on Waterlow as he bathed, she wrote, "My God! what a sight he looked bathing! like Neptune, if Neptune was a Eunuch! – without any hairs, and sky pink – fresh, virginal, soft – I sat on the bank and peered through the rushes."

21. G. C. Beresford, *Thoby Stephen*
August 1906

Reprinted by permission of the Harvard Theatre Collection, The Houghton Library

This photo was taken of Thoby Stephen shortly before he left for Greece where, on the trip with his siblings, he would contract the typhoid fever that would fell him permanently months later. He died on November 20 of that year, at the age of 26. Despite Virginia's grief, she pretended to Violet Dickinson, herself recovering from the same illness, that he was doing well, hoping that this news would spur the recovery of her friend. His death had a different effect on Vanessa, his elder sister. Two days after Thoby's death she agreed to marry Clive, whose proposals she had previously rebuffed. Virginia composed *Jacob's Room* in part to honor his life and memory, and after completion of *The Waves* she confided in her diary: "sitting these 15 minutes in a state of glory, & calm, & some tears, thinking of Thoby & if I could write Julian Thoby Stephen 1881-1906 on the first page. I suppose not." She wrote to Vanessa, "I have a dumb rage still at his not being with us always."[22] Vanessa responded that with *The Waves*, "if you wouldn't think me foolish I should say that you have found the 'lullaby capable of singing him to rest.'"[23]

22. Thoby Stephen, *Compulsory Chapel*

Cambridge: Privately printed, 1904
Private collection

First – and only – edition of this pamphlet anonymously printed and privately circulated by Thoby among his Cambridge cohorts. Described on the cover as an "appeal to undergraduates on behalf of religious liberty and intellectual independence," it bears the following legend from Horace at the foot of that page: "Vidi ergo civium / Retorta tergo brachia libero" – "I have seen the citizens' arms twisted back behind their backs; therefore I am setting them free."
Addressing himself "to the Freshmen of Cambridge University," he writes,

> [W]ith you rests our chief hope of purging our Republic of bigotry and intolerance; that yours is the power and yours the opportunity of making a worthy stand in the cause of Freedom of Opinion and Independence in Religious practices. For those who now enter either of our Universities have at least this privilege which is denied to their countrymen elsewhere, that they are compelled for once to make a clear choice between bowing to the illegal authority of hoary prejudice or asserting the rightful independence of their intellectual manhood. (3)

He sketches the legal history of their freedom of religion, and laments that he and his classmates "now seem too feeble even to enjoy the fruits of" the victory of their predecessors (4).

He continues to support his argument with examples of undeniable religious intolerance: that there are no lay heads or deans of college; that chapel attendance is compulsory, and failure to meet this obligation results in punishment; that entering freshmen are bullied into attending, their rights not made plain to them, their dissention ignored, and punishment tacitly threatened if rebellion is scented. "It was in reference to this line of action that I used the word *illegal* in my first paragraph. For though deans may keep within the letter of the law when they compel all those who do not definitely associate themselves with some other recognized creed to attend the Chapel services, I maintain that in acting thus they plainly outrage its spirit" (6).

His final salvo is directed at the undergraduates themselves, for "the law gives them their independence, if they will have the courage and the energy to insist upon their rights:

> Could anything degrade a free man more than that he should condescend week after week to fabricate excuses for not attending a religious service which he dislikes or despises? Is there any more pestilential phenomenon than the fictitious crops of pleurisies, rheums, and sciaticas that is bred by each Cambridge Sunday? If in truth apathy and ignorance rather than cowardice are the roots of the evil I may hope to do some good by putting before you this plain statement of your position. But we cannot maintain the right of free thinking unless we are prepared to recognize the duty of Plain Speaking. Believing this I appeal not only to Atheists and Agnostics, but to all friends of intellectual independence, and to those Christians – if such there be – who consider that compulsory worship is an indignity to themselves and to their creed. They will have on their side not only the law, but the whole weight of enlightened opinion outside the University. I am pointing them to no forlorn hope, no quest for the impossible. The prize is ready to the hand of all but the sluggard and the craven. (7-8)

23. Virginia Woolf, *Jacob's Room*

Richmond: The Hogarth Press, 1922
Private collection

First edition of her first novel to appear under the Hogarth Press imprint; in addition to five pages of ads, nine pages of reviews of Virginia's earlier works appear in the rear; 1200 copies printed. (Kirkpatrick A6a, Woolmer 26)

Described by one critic as an "elegy for the generation of men that was slaughtered in World War I," but by others as a tribute to Thoby Stephen, who died in 1906 and who was openly associated with the character of Jacob upon publication, *Jacob's Room* was Woolf's first stylistic watershed. After she finished it, she declared, "There's no doubt in my mind that I have found out how to begin (at 40) to say something in my own voice; & that interests me so that I feel I can go ahead without praise." That voice had evolved out of literary experiments such as "An Unwritten Novel," "The Mark on the Wall," and "Kew Gardens," as she had prophesied it would over two years before:

> [T]his afternoon arrived at some idea of a new form for a new novel. Suppose one thing should open out of another – as in An Unwritten Novel – only not for 10 pages but 200 or so – doesn't that give the looseness & lightness I want: doesn't that get closer & yet keep form & speed, & enclose everything, everything? My doubt is how far it will <include> enclose the human heart – Am I sufficiently mistress of my dialogue to net it there? For I figure that the approach will be entirely different this time; no scaffolding; scarcely a brick to be seen; all crepuscular, but the heart, the passion, humour, everything as bright as fire in the mist . Indeed, I think from the ease with which I'm developing the unwritten novel there must be a path for me there.

Virginia's friends unanimously hailed *Jacob's Room* as a contribution to the creation of a new literary form.

24. (Geddes) Paul Hyslop, *Lytton Strachey*

Ca. late 1920s
Courtesy Abbott and Holder Ltd.

From the photograph album compiled by (Geddes) Paul Hyslop, the lover and companion of Hogarth Press author, *New Statesman and Nation* editor, and recipient of Virginia's thanks in her preface to *Orlando*, Raymond Mortimer.

A founding member of the Midnight Society and the *X* Society, two play-reading groups at Cambridge, and a close friend of their core members – Leonard, Clive, Thoby, and Saxon Sydney-Turner – Giles Lytton Strachey was secretary of the Apostles, a post that would consume him for his final three years at Cambridge. In 1904 Leonard left Cambridge for service in Ceylon. Meanwhile, Strachey remained in England, writing for the *Spectator*, falling in love with his cousin, Duncan Grant, and developing a friendship with the Stephen siblings at 46 Gordon Square. His intimacy with Virginia led to a moment-long engagement, which both thought better of as soon as the words were spoken.

By the time Leonard returned to London in 1911, Lytton was well established in literary circles, able to identify new talents to channel into the Bloomsbury Group and eventually through the Hogarth Press. Virginia captured her earliest views of Lytton in the character of St. John Hirst in *The Voyage Out*. In 1918 he published *Eminent Victorians*, and so defined his own career in debunking the moral and aesthetic philosophies of their forebears. Throughout her career Woolf depended on Strachey to render honest criticism of her works. She also took great pleasure in critiquing, and appreciating, his writing. She wrote in 1924, "Why do I always fly to your works when the electricians are in the hall, the gasmen in the basement, and the telephone ringing with Tom's [T. S. Eliot's] sepulchral voice? It's a very queer fact, but in moments of crisis, I always turn to you but supply me with another book soon."[24] Over the years they wrote each other with less and less frequency, but with no less affection.

25. Lytton Strachey, *Autograph letter signed to Virginia*
October 9, 1922

Virginia Woolf, *Autograph letter signed to Lytton*
October 9, 1922

Mortimer Rare Book Room, Smith College

In these letters, both dated October 9, 1922, Lytton offers his thoughts on *Jacob's Room* and Virginia delights in it in her reply. "More like poetry, it seems to me, than anything else, and as such I prophecy immortal," Lytton writes. "The technique of the narrative is astonishing I occasionally almost screamed with joy at the writing . Jacob himself I think is very successful – in a most remarkable &' original way. Of course I see something of Thoby in him, as I supposed was intended." David Garnett, Desmond, Clive, and Edwin Muir concurred in their reviews. She replied to Lytton with some apprehension: "I can't believe you really like a work so utterly devoid of so many virtues; but it gives me immense pleasure to dream that you do." She also addressed the source of his one complaint: "Of course you put your infallible finger upon the spot – romanticism... some of it, I think, comes from the effort of breaking with complete representation. One flies into the air. Next time, I mean to stick closer to facts." Four years passed before E. M. Forster made his pronouncement, but it would be worth the wait: "The coherence of the book is even more amazing than its beauty . The break with *Night and Day* and even with *The Voyage Out* is complete. A new type of fiction has swum into view ."

26. Leonard Woolf

Ceylon, ca. 1904-11

Reprinted by permission of the Harvard Theatre Collection, The Houghton Library

In 1904, Leonard joined the Ceylon Civil Service, "taking with him a fox terrier and seventy volumes of Voltaire."[25] Seven years later he returned, on furlough, in disgust, repulsed by his country's colonial practices in Sri Lanka and by his own complicity. Fifty years later he would publish *Growing*, his memoir of those years, but it wouldn't take that long to immortalize his experiences in print: in 1911 he fictionalized his experiences, narrating the horrors of imperialism through the eyes of the natives in *The Village in the Jungle*.

III. Bloomsbury in Love

George Duckworth, *Leonard Woolf and Virginia Stephen*
Dalingridge Place, July 23, 1912, three weeks before their marriage
Reprinted by permission of the Harvard Theatre Collection, The Houghton Library

Love in Bloomsbury by William Beekman

Bloomsbury is famous (or notorious) for its frank talk of love and sex (in "Old Bloomsbury," prepared for the Memoir Club, Virginia recalled Lytton Strachey, upon entering the drawing room of the newlywed Mr. and Mrs. Clive Bell, pointing at a stain on Vanessa's white dress and asking, "Semen?"). However, even though "all barriers of reserve and reticence went down" (again, from "Old Bloomsbury"), Virginia Woolf and her group nonetheless expressed and enjoyed all of the usual types of love, as exemplified by the objects in this show.

The expression "Bloomsbury Group" was coined in the '30s and perhaps implied a type of affiliation based on elective affinity (as opposed to an expression like School of Paris, which only suggests a common discipline or aesthetic). Indeed, insofar as the Bloomsbury Group had a shared philosophy it was undoubtedly derived from G. E. Moore, who spoke of the bonds of human affection, love, and sex as positive goods.

Sister Love

Virginia's letter to Vanessa on the occasion of her marriage to Clive, teasing and playful, suggests a childish intimacy. Yet at the time Virginia was 24 and Vanessa was 27, hardly children. Virginia was working at her career as author, and it is clear from the penmanship as well as the content that the letter was conceived and written with care but (almost certainly) without any expectation of scrutiny by posterity. The letter is coded and humorous and addresses Vanessa with affection as a fellow conspirator, and it promises to welcome Clive as a third member of the conspiracy.

Yet the letter has an elegiac tone as well. Clearly Virginia understood that Vanessa and Clive were embarking on a new kind of intimate relationship, one that would necessarily exclude her. Instead of having the "red ape" join the menagerie, he was truly carrying her "mistress" off to a new site, where they would make a home together and Virginia would be welcome only by invitation. Yet Virginia and Vanessa's love for each other was to endure, and their closeness to be established on a new plane of adult life, as collaborators, neighbors, helpmates, and (yes) sisters. Vanessa would come to assist in the case of Virginia's "nervous collapses," and Virginia would be doting aunt to Vanessa's children, as well as Vanessa's nurse and helpmeet at the time of the sudden death of Julian, Vanessa's oldest son, in the Spanish Civil War.

Gallant Love

Clive Bell's poem, written to V[irginia] S[tephen] around the time of their flirtation and subsequently published with other poems for all the world (or at least his private subscription list) to see, shows a fine sensibility trained on the object of his desire. The poem is addressed to his once-beloved; does she

> Recall the pregnant hours, the gay delights,
> The pain, the tears maybe, the ravished heights,
> The golden moments my cold lines commend,
> The days, in memory of which I send
> A book?

The poem addresses "VS" in courteous terms, vesting the book that he proffers as a token of his remembered, but evidently past, love with emotional heft and significance. Who knows which book it might have been, but the air of formal intimacy, almost eighteenth century in character, is very tangible.

Clive Bell was perhaps the closest of the Bloomsbury Group to a conventional character from a nineteenth-century novel. His amours and escapades were at once gentlemanly and hurtful (at least in the beginning) to his wife. Ultimately, he and Vanessa arrived at an arrangement and essentially led their separate lives while remaining in close touch. It could be argued that Vanessa's life with Duncan Grant, who remained actively homosexual, was innovative, but probably only because there is scant evidence of similar arrangements in previous, less thoroughly documented times. But Clive was a happy heterosexual of a certain class and while he was a central figure in the Bloomsbury Group, and is still remembered for influential works of art criticism, his social life, including his amorous life, was hardly innovative.

Marital Love

Virginia Woolf was famously uninterested in, possibly even averse to, sexual intimacy, at least with men. Leonard Woolf's autobiography, so frank in every other respect, does not really discuss how he coped with her physical remoteness. After he establishes his own virile credentials (discussing sex with a prostitute in Ceylon), he dismisses the whole category of sexual intimacy as if it were a mere detail of gross bodily function.

Notwithstanding the apparent (and much discussed) lack of a "normal" sexual relationship, Leonard and Virginia's marriage was famously close and has withstood the scrutiny of even the most antagonistic critics. His dedication to his then-new wife in *Village in the Jungle* is eloquent, tender, and modest. Other inscriptions in surviving books from their library bespeak a continuing closeness and (despite the vagaries of Virginia's mental state) devotion. If he had any active sexual relations with other women during their marriage, it did not appear to affect their own relationship in any adverse manner.

Sexual Love

With the publication of biographies and letters in the frank-speaking days of the 1970s, the Bloomsbury Group became famous for its "free love," "open marriage" lifestyle. One demographic of the group that bears remembering is the gay men in the circle (referred to as "buggers" by Virginia), who enjoyed a somewhat promiscuous and episodic series of sexual relationships. But Vanessa, second only to Virginia as the leading woman of Bloomsbury, had her own "open marriage" with Clive, settling into a passionate relationship with Roger Fry before taking up a close domestic (and at least occasionally sexual) relationship with Duncan Grant, the father of her daughter Angelica and an active "bugger." The photograph of Vanessa on the rocky shore (or in a quarry), wearing nothing but a pair of shoes and a hat or scarf, was apparently taken by Roger Fry and probably dates from a period after the end of their sexual relationship. Despite the oddness of the evidently civilized woman standing there in that rocky landscape hiding nothing, the image does not appear to be intended as pornographic or even provocative.

Vanessa appears serenely confident and evidently not at all self-conscious. The image bespeaks sexual love because of the one-time relationship of the two participants, photographer and subject, as well as because of the subject's own matter-of-factness about her situation: wife, mother, artist, respectable, and nude. Indeed, from today's vantage Vanessa Bell appears to be a prophet of a feminist lifestyle that would come to popularity in the latter quarter of the twentieth century, a proudly independent and self-sufficient sexual woman: a body of one's own.

Sapphic Love

Vita Sackville-West was not an original member of the Bloomsbury Group, and (because of her high birth and grand manner of living) one might quibble about whether she was a member at all. In any case, by the time she met Virginia, she was already somewhat notorious as a free-living aristocrat with an open marriage and a taste for women. Of course, all of this was to be explored in detail by her son in his book *Portrait of a Marriage*, published in the 1970s to great acclaim and some prurient interest.

When Vita and Virginia first met through Clive Bell, each, in her own way, was already famous. Virginia had heard gossip of Vita's sexual escapades, and Vita had read and admired Virginia's novels (Vita herself being at that time already a bestselling author). Initially somewhat reticent or even timid, Virginia eventually fell into an intimate and active friendship with Vita, evidently with Leonard's blessing. Vita wrote poetry as well as novels, and on view are two manuscript poems expressing the passion and jealousy inspired by Virginia. Also on display is a playful letter from Leonard, commending Virginia to Vita's care as if she were a dog being sent off to board.

One of Vita's poems ("Your darkened windows numb my darkened heart") recalls her jealousy looking down on Virginia Woolf's bedroom window ("I look in vain across the sable night, / and rage against our separate life apart"). The language is both poetically overwrought ("sable night") and urgent ("Where are you gone? Who seeing? Where, oh where / Loved stranger, daily but elusive friend . . . ?"). Finally, the poem's third stanza resolves itself in a victorious declaration:

> —Only, tonight my heart may triumph keep:
> Your golden casement suffers its eclipse,
> But it was I who dimmed your lights to sleep
> And left you with my kiss upon your lips.

It is a poem of jealousy and romantic conquest, recalling male poets of a prior age. The other poem ("I remember, she told me once at Vezelay") is both less archaic and less awkward, but also less finished. It is based on a trip the two women took together, and the memory of a thunderstorm that frightened Virginia: "she came into my room / Shivering there with fright, and lay with me." The account takes on a mystical tone ("She talked that night of immortality"), and then resolves itself, or is perhaps rewritten, as follows:

> I shall never forget that night
> When Virginia told me in Vezelay about her belief in immortality
> And about the pin that Walter Pater's sister dropped
> From a red rose ~~on to a table~~
> Spilling the petals of the red rose onto the table
> When she was teaching Greek to Virginia
>
>   [two blank lines]
>
> The tiny pin and the great thunderstorm.

This is not a poem of romantic conquest but of primal and unexplained emotion, alternating between the references of the genteel, scholarly world in which Virginia Woolf was raised (Walter Pater's sister taught her Greek) and the wild weather, the red rose (red as blood) and the thunderstorm.

Lifeforce Love

G. E. Moore was the mentor and role model for the thinking men of Bloomsbury, and he believed in the affinity of kindred spirits based on shared ideas and admiration of physical beauty. In *Principia Ethica* he stated the principle that "personal affections and aesthetic enjoyments include all the greatest, and *by far* the greatest, goods we can imagine" (189). The Cambridge Apostles (and their Cambridge friends) who comprised the men of Bloomsbury were imbued with his ideas, and those ideas seeped out and affected the women as well. Thus, Virginia Woolf's diary entry, from which the title of this show is taken, while an original observation, is certainly influenced by Moore's ideas of love as a positive, or even essential, social good.

"Our loving" is a constant, unifying theme within the groupings within the Bloomsbury Group. As discussed, the Group members enjoyed many types of love between and among themselves. Their loves were not always happy (witness Carrington and Lytton), but they were sincere and, frequently, intense. Except, perhaps, for Clive, the love they felt for each other was hardly ever the stuff of a Cole Porter lyric. To grab another improbable (and anachronistic) cultural reference, their love was more attuned, perhaps, to the Lennon and McCartney of "All You Need Is Love." One explanation for the continuing fascination of the Bloomsbury Group is this protean and shared sense of love, which combines the elements of the familiar and the novel, the healthy and the neurotic, the "normal" and the "abnormal." It is hard to deny the appeal of these brave, passionate, and occasionally misguided individuals in their couplings and other well-documented interactions.

27. Virginia Stephen, *Autograph engagement announcement, to Lytton Strachey*

June 6, 1912

Mortimer Rare Book Room, Smith College

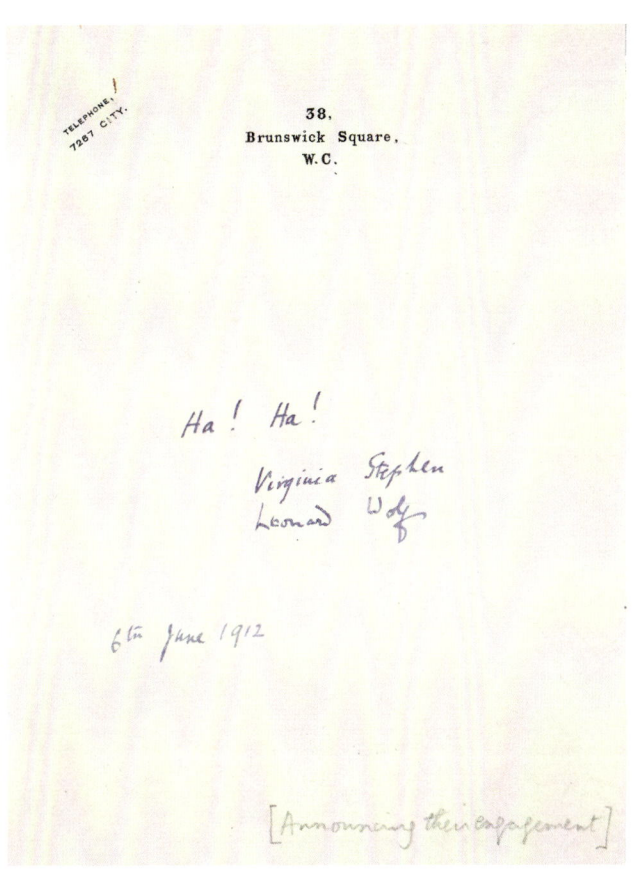

Virginia writes to Lytton announcing her engagement to Leonard: the note reads in full, "Ha! Ha! Virginia Stephen. Leonard Woolf." Lytton and Virginia had developed a close friendship during Leonard's years in Ceylon, but as soon as Lytton proposed he and Virginia both knew it was not to be. He described the situation to his brother James on March 9, 1909: "On February 19th I proposed to Virginia, and was accepted. It was an awkward moment, as you may imagine, especially as I realized, the very minute it was happening, that the whole thing was repulsive to me. Her sense was amazing, and luckily it turned out that she's not in love. The result was that I was able to manage a fairly honourable retreat. The story is really rather amusing and singular, but its effect has been to drive me on to these shoals more furiously than ever. I need hardly mention the immense secrecy of the affair ." Virginia assured Molly MacCarthy a few years later: "No, I shan't float into a bloodless alliance with Lytton – though he is in some ways perfect as a friend, only he's a female friend."[26]

In 1912 Leonard resigned his government post in Ceylon in favor of a clean political conscience and marriage to Virginia, on August 10, 1912. By then over a decade had passed since their first meeting, but their courtship was brief but intense. He moved in to Brunswick Square in December 1911, renting a room from Virginia and Adrian; in January 1912 he tendered his proposal. She had many concerns, some of which had led her to reject offers from three previous suitors. Leonard's was the first to which she gave serious consideration. She wrote to him on May 1:

> I will not look upon marriage as a profession . Possibly, your being a Jew comes in also at this point. You seem so foreign. And then I am fearfully unstable . So I go from being half in love with you, and wanting you to be with me always, and know everything about me, to the extreme of wildness and aloofness. I sometimes think that if I married you, I could have everything – and then – is it the sexual side of it that comes between us? As I told you brutally the other day, I feel no physical attraction in you. There are moments – when you kissed me the other day was one – when I feel no more than a rock.

But the encouragement she offered him, in that same letter, was enough to convince him to remain in England to press his suit:

> All I can say is that in spite of these feelings which go chasing each other all day long when I am with you, there is some feeling which is permanent, and growing your caring for me as you do almost overwhelms me. But it's just because you care so much that I feel I've got to care before I marry you. I feel I must give you everything; and that if I can't, well, marriage would only be second-best for you as well as for me. We both of us want a marriage that is a tremendous living thing, always alive, always hot, not dead and easy in parts as most marriages are.

By month's end she had accepted him, and sent notes full of wit and joy to her closest friends, whom she hoped would come to know and like this "penniless Jew": "I'm more happy than anyone ever said was possible. Leonard is far and away the most interesting and charming man I know, and I feel that I shall have to increase in virtue as his wife. It's not at all what people say, but so much better. I don't think I'm nearly worth what he is. I'm very happy – and find him more necessary every day." She includes in most of these missives some reassurance that their marriage will not be typical. "L. thinks my writing the best part of me. We're going to work very hard. We mean to do quantities of things. L. wants me to say that if I cease to write when married, I shall be divorced."[27] She sent a lengthier letter to Madge Symonds Vaughan:

> First he is a Jew: second he is 31; third, he spent 7 years in Ceylon, governing natives, inventing ploughs, shooting tigers, and did so well that they offered him a very high place the other day, which he refused, wishing to marry me, . . . He has no money on his own. He has been living at Brunswick Sq. [with Virginia and Adrian] since December – we know each other as I imagine few people do before marriage. I've only known him 6 months, but from the first I have found him the one person to talk to. He has also written a novel, and means to write as well as be practical. We shall, I think, take a small house and try to live cheaply, so as not to have to make money.[28]

28. Leonard Woolf, *The Village in the Jungle*

London: Edward Arnold, 1913
Private collection

First edition of Leonard's first novel. The dedication copy, inscribed on the dedication page beneath the printed dedication: *Leonard. / 20 Feb 1913*. The printed dedication reads,

> To V.W.
>
> I've given you all the little, that I've to give;
> You've given me all, that for me is all there is;
> So now I just give back what you have given—
> If there is anything to give in this.

A cornerstone document of the relationship between Leonard and Virginia Woolf.

The first years of the Woolfs' marriage were marked by their individual creative endeavors. By the time of the ceremony Virginia was nearly ready to submit *The Voyage Out* to George Duckworth, and

Leonard had completed *The Village in the Jungle*. Drawing on his experience in Ceylon and his distaste for England's position there, it was "a genuine original, an account of small-village life that re-creates plausibly and powerfully, yet somewhat vicariously, the natives' fears and vulnerabilities in the face of a hostile environment and an alien administration that fails to understand them even when it seeks to provide care and justice."[29] Living on Virginia's small but sufficient income, he completed a second – *The Wise Virgins* (1915), in which he fictionalized elements of their relationship. When neither of these novels saw a fraction of the critical or commercial success for which he had hoped, Leonard rededicated himself to politics and to the editorial work on which his reputation ultimately rested.

Virginia, meanwhile, had her own first two novels published by Duckworth: *The Voyage Out* (1915) and *Night and Day* (1919). Her renown as a critical mind had already been established through her political work and book reviews, and her creative reputation soon caught up. But her emotional instability increased markedly. Virginia's mental state was known to her family and guessed at within their immediate circle, but even Leonard was not aware of the extent of her debility until after the wedding. Sexually abused as an adolescent by her half-brothers; bereft at the age of 13 when her mother died and, in her early twenties, when her half-sister, then her father, and then her brother passed away, she had suffered several breakdowns and survived one suicide attempt. Leonard sought advice from several professionals, and decided, on her behalf, against children, adding more strain to her already considerable load. With the purchase of their first printing press in 1917, the Hogarth Press was born. However, the child question is one that Virginia turned over in her mind repeatedly and painfully throughout her life.

The inner character of the marriage of Virginia and Leonard Woolf – what it was, or came to be – cannot be ascertained, though scholars have long and hotly debated the subject and will continue to do so. This volume, a witness to the earliest, arguably happiest days of their union, numbers first among a handful of relics quietly testifying to the truth of their relationship.

29. William Congreve, *The Works*

Dublin: Thomas Ewing, 1773
Private collection

An early collected edition. A Christmas gift from Leonard to Virginia, inscribed in volume one on the front paste-down: *Virginia Woolf from L.W. 25/12/22 Rodmell*. This set was a timely gift to Virginia, who had reviewed a performance of Congreve's *Love for Love* for *New Statesmen* in 1921, beginning a lasting critical relationship with his works. She anonymously reviewed the revised edition of Gosse's *The Life of William Congreve*, along with Bonamy Dobrée's *Restoration Comedy* for the *New Republic* in February 1925, and anonymously reviewed *The Comedies of William Congreve*, published by Oxford University Press, that fall in *Nation & Atheneum*. Her 1937 *TLS* essay "Congreve's Comedies: Speed, Stillness and Meaning" was reprinted in *The Moment and Other Essays* in 1947 and in *Collected Essays Volume One* in 1966. In it, she writes, "to read Congreve's plays is to be convinced that we may learn from them many lessons much to our advantage both as writers of books and – if the division is possible – as livers of life."

She goes on to tackle several criticisms lodged against him; for example, "Undoubtedly it is true that his language is often coarse; but then it is also true that his characters are more alive, quicker to strip off veils, more intolerant of circumlocutions than the ordinary run of people." What is more, he has "a genius for phrase-making."

Woolf's admiration for elements of Congreve's work are traced by Hussey: "In *Night and Day*, seeing Katharine Hilbery approach as he waits to meet her in Kew Gardens, Ralph Denham thinks that she comes 'like a ship in full sail.' The line is from Congreve's *The Way of the World*, a play that Woolf often alludes to . In the play, Millamant and Mirabell establish unconventional guidelines for their friendship in a way similar to that Ralph and Katharine work out during their conversation at Kew."[30]

30. Thomas Love Peacock, *The Misfortunes of Elphin*

London: Thomas Hookham, 1829
Private collection

First edition of this parody of the Arthurian legend. A Christmas gift, inscribed on the front endpaper: *V.W. from L.W. Christmas 1911 August 1936*. With a couplet from the book:

> Unlooked for good betides us still
> And unanticipated ill.

Leonard altered the years in the inscription from 1912 and 1937 by superimposing a "1" and a "6" in the same ink. Lee notes that this inscription "referred eloquently to their long companionship and to their present sadness. For her, their work and their marriage were her two most profound resources. At times to come – as at times in the past – she would think of their old inseparability not as an achievement but as a failure, a bondage, a form of 'damnable servility'. But now, not being able to part – when she thought of joining Nessa, who had gone to Paris in October, she then decided she could not go without him – was a great consolation."

Peacock (1785-1866) was best known for his satirical novels, the first of which – *Headlong Hall* – was easily the most popular. Forster saw "something of" Peacock's humor in *The Voyage Out*. In February 1922 Woolf re-read two Peacock novels she had not opened since her youth: *Nightmare Abbey* and *Crochet Castle*. She noted in her diary how her responses had changed, and how Peacock's works caused her to reflect on her own writing:

> Both are so much better than I remember. Doubtless, Peacock is a taste acquired in maturity. When I was young, reading him in a railway carriage in Greece, sitting opposite Thoby, I remember, who pleased me immensely by approving my remark that Meredith had got his women from Peacock, & that they were very charming women, then, I say I rather had to prod my enthusiasm. Thoby liked it straight off. I wanted mystery, romance, psychology I suppose. And now more than anything I want beautiful prose. I relish it more & more exquisitely. And I enjoy satire more. I like the skepticism of his mind more. I enjoy intellectuality. Moreover, fantasticality does a good deal better than sham psychology. One touch of red in the cheek is all he gives, but I can do the rest. And then they're so short; & I read them in little yellowish perfectly appropriate first editions.

Days later she wrote, "My only interest as a writer lies, I begin to see, in some queer individuality: not in strength, or passion, or anything startling; but then I say to myself, is not 'some queer individuality' precisely the quality I respect? Peacock, for example: Borrow; Donne; Douglas, in Alone, has a touch of it . People with this gift of on sounding long after the melodious vigorous music is banal." That fall, she compared Vanessa's prospective living arrangements with a Peacock work: "Maynard is going to build a house: N. & D. are going to draw an income for 10 years from it. It is to be a hotel, perfectly appointed, in a field off Beanstalk Lane – 8 suites of rooms, with 8 bathrooms, kitchens, waterclosets, surrounding a courtyard; in short a Peacock novel in stone; soon filled with the characters."
A diary entry in August 1928 suggests she planned to write on Peacock, but if she did, that essay goes unrecorded.

31. Virginia Woolf and Leonard Woolf, *Two Stories*
Richmond: The Hogarth Press, 1917
Private collection

First edition of the first publication of the Hogarth Press, printing "Three Jews" by Leonard and "The Mark on the Wall" by Virginia. Four woodcuts by Dora Carrington appear throughout the text – two for each story – but no credit is ascribed. They printed 150 copies, and bound them in whatever paper they had to hand: copies in blue wrappers are most common; then the red and white patterned covers; copies in yellow wrappers are scarce; other variations exist. This earliest production from the Hogarth Press reflects their early investment in it as a hobby. The creation of the Hogarth Press was an act of love on Leonard's part, to help Virginia maintain mental stability. The joint venture, in its earliest stage, took the place, in some ways, of a child; later it became a legitimate business partnership.

32. Virginia Stephen, *Autograph letter to Vanessa*
February 6, 1907
Private collection

Writing to Vanessa on the eve of her marriage to Clive Bell, Virginia expresses in this playful note her love of her sister and her approval of her fiancé. She signs the letter collectively as Vanessa's "devoted Beasts," apes named Bartholomew, Mungo, and Wombat, each in a different hand. "Wombat"

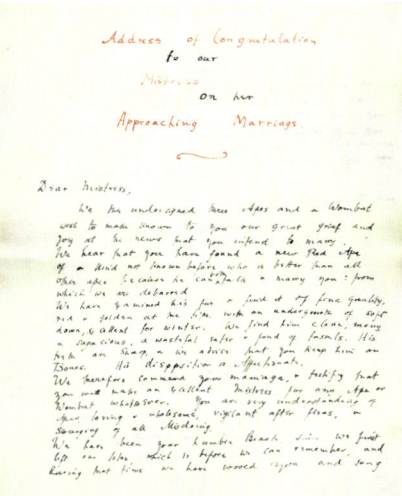
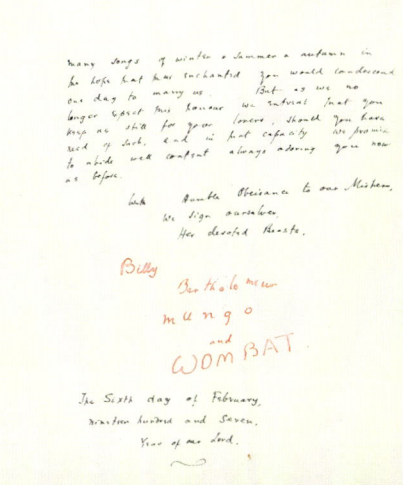

would remind Vanessa of the character about whom they wove tales in their youth. She writes that Clive is a "new Red Ape of a kind not known before who is better than all other apes because he can both talk and marry you: from which we are debarred." In addition to this, he is "clean, merry, and sagacious, a wasteful eater and fond of fossils . His disposition is Affectionate."

> We therefore commend your marriage, and testify that you will make an excellent Mistress for any Ape or Wombat whatsoever. You are very understanding of Apes, loving and wholesome, vigilant after fleas, and scourging of all Misdoing.

She sends, with affection, her love and devotion that will not end at her marriage, promising "to abide well content always adoring you now as before" and signing off "With Humble Obeisance to our Mistress."

33. Vanessa Stephen, *Virginia Stephen and Clive Bell*
Studland
1910
Private collection

Years after Clive, Thoby's best friend at Cambridge, wed Vanessa in 1907, Clive had a fairly intense flirtation with Virginia, around the time of this photo, before her marriage to Leonard in 1912. Vanessa, mothering her first son, was initially upset by the relationship, but equilibrium was reestablished in due course. Soon after, Clive began a series of full-blown affairs. Later in the year this photo was taken, Vanessa began a relationship with Roger Fry, whom she left after a few years to live with Duncan Grant. She later adopted a tolerant, affectionate, and slightly condescending attitude toward Clive and his lady friends. For his part, Clive became more of a visitor than a proprietor at the homes of his wife and family.

For the excursion depicted in this photo, to Studland in Dorset, Virginia sports rented swimwear: "I hired a gentlemans or ladies – it was bisexual – a bathing dress, and swam far out a drifting sea anemone." She writes of the holiday: "Julian rushes straight into the sea, and falls flat on his face. Nessa tucks her skirts up, and wades about with him. Clive meanwhile dives from a boat, in a tight black suit."[31]

34. Clive Bell, *"To V.S. With a Book"*

In *Ad Familiares*
London: Printed by Francis Meynell at the Pelican Press, October 1917
Ottoline Morrell's copy
Private collection

Clive, while married to Vanessa, writes a love poem to Virginia describing the intense emotion he attaches to sending her a book. It reads in full:

Books are the quiet monitor of mind,
They prompt its motions, shape its ways, they find
A road through mazes to the higher ground,
Whence to explore the sky-bound marches.
Round
about us lie the open downs. Our days
Still ask a guide and goad. Wherefore always
We meditate wise thoughts and passionate lays;
Wherefore I send a book.

Books are the mind's last symbol. They express
Its visions and its subtleties – a dress
Material for the immaterial things
That soar to immortality on wings
Of words, and live, by magic of the pen,
Where dead minds live, upon the lips of men
And deep in hearts that stir. Wherefore do I,
Drawing a little near, prophetically,
Send you a book.

Books are the heart's memorial. They shall measure,
In after days, our undiscovered treasure, –
Thrilling self-knowledge, half-divined untold
Yearnings, and tongueless agonies, shall unfold
Or half unfold to half-illumined eyes.
The cypress shadows creeping gnomonwise
Still stretch their purple fingers down the hill
That hangs above Fiesole; and still
Your English fireside glows. Do you most dear
 – Sometimes just guessed at, sometimes very near –
Yet always dear and fairest friend, do you
Recall the sunlight and the firelight too?
Recall the pregnant hours, the gay delights,
The pain, the tears maybe, the ravished heights,
The golden moments my cold lines commend,
The days, in memory of which I send
A book?

Dec. 1909

35. *Vanessa Bell, Clive Bell, and Duncan Grant*

Ca. 1917
Reprinted by permission of the Harvard Theatre Collection, The Houghton Library

Some scholars place Lytton's effervescent, alluring cousin Duncan Grant at the center of the Bloomsbury Group. The early object of Lytton's affection, he lived, at various times, with Adrian Stephen, and John Maynard Keynes, and David "Bunny" Garnett (and had affairs with all three), Virginia, and Leonard, and Vanessa, with whom he had the longest intimate working and personal relationship. Duncan and Vanessa modeled for each other's sketches and paintings; they collaborated on work for Roger Fry's Omega Workshops and on their own.
Their styles were deeply involved with one another's, and even now authorship is questioned on a number of artworks. In 1916 they moved to Charleston, where two years later their daughter Angelica was born (though subsequently raised as Clive's child until she learned the truth at the age of 17).

36. Ottoline Morrell, *Virginia Woolf and Lytton Strachey*

Garsington, June 1923

Reprinted by permission of the Harvard Theatre Collection, The Houghton Library

Humorously captioned by Virginia in the Monk's House Album *Lytton Strachey & Yeats at Ottoline Morrell's*, it includes Goldsworthy Lowes Dickinson, as well, at the far end of the bench (eclipsed here). Ottoline, an object of occasional condescension and gentle mockery among the Bloomsbury set, was a socialite with literary aspirations who hosted frequent literary parties and salons for her arch friends.

37. Virginia Woolf, *Autograph letters signed to Lytton Strachey*

Boxing Day 1912, September 8, 1925

Mortimer Rare Book Room, Smith College

Virginia writes in the earlier letter from Asheham, Rodmell, where she lived with Leonard, of their move to the country – a decision Leonard made for her health, and one that proved a mixed blessing for her; about Christmas Eve, and her thoughts on their mutual friend Ottoline Morrell; and about Vanessa and Roger Fry, with allusions to their affair, their work at his Omega Workshops, and their recovery from the Post-Impressionist exhibit of 1912. She writes as a youthful and catty confidante, sharing glimpses of the whirlwind she inhabits:

> I meant long ago to write to you, in London, but one can't write in London. In fact we're driven to think that the country is our destiny.
>
> We have just had dinner – Leonard is reading the poems of John Donne: I am half way through the Return of the Native, a novel by Thomas Hardy. We go back tomorrow, alas. Were there time I would tell you about Brighton on Christmas Eve; we spent 2 hours in the Aquarium. For some reason, the mackerel put me in mind of Ottoline and her troupe; she ought to be put in a tank; it's absurd to expect her to stand scrutiny for ways and motives, which is her lot at present.
>
> I suppose you have heard of various disasters in London – Nessa more or less broken down – Roger rampant, but at one point forced to sit with his head in his hands, giddy if he so much as saw a picture. They're starting on furniture now – have you heard? All good reasons for living in the country.

In the second letter, she writes as an older, wiser friend, one who reflects now more than she gossips. She acknowledges they don't keep in touch as they used to, but reminds him of the importance of his friendship – not to mention of his critical acumen. In preparation for a new edition of her *Common Reader*, she asks for his thoughts, and concludes by reminding him of their closeness, no matter how much time passes: "Do you remember one of Leslie Stephen's daughters, the younger, I think, called Virginia? Find me a house where no one can ever come. I like talking to you, but to no one else in the whole world. Your old, rake, and fireside hag, V."

IV. The Visual Arts in Bloomsbury

Vanessa Bell, *Study for The Memoir Club,* ca. 1943
Private collection
© The Estate of Vanessa Bell, courtesy Henrietta Garnett

The Arrival of Post-Impressionism in Bloomsbury by Rachel Cohen

It was a cold morning in January, a Monday, in 1910, and Clive and Vanessa Bell (she had been Bell for just three years now, having accepted his second proposal, two days after her brother's death) were taking a train from Cambridge to London. In the station she saw a man whom she knew slightly, and, with some trepidation, went up to greet him. Once in the train car, Roger Fry brought out his manuscript, but instead fell fully into conversation with the hearty and likeable Clive Bell, whose time living in Paris had familiarized him with the developments in painting Fry was then most "on about," namely the way the revolutions in French painting had continued beyond Impressionism to be seen in new forms in the works of Cézanne, Van Gogh, Gauguin, and now, breaking ever forward, in those of Matisse, Picasso, Derain, Rouault. Fry, leaping, as always, among plans, observations, and theories, put forward his idea of having an art show to educate the thus-far ignorant British public. Frances Spalding, in *Roger Fry: Art and Life,* quotes the two Bells in their different reactions. "When Roger Fry told me that morning that he proposed to show the British public the work of the newest French painters," and you can hear Clive Bell's fond amusement, "I told him that I would be proud to help in any way I could but that his scheme was fantastic."[32] Vanessa Bell's reaction was also characteristic:

> As he sat opposite me in the corner I looked at his face bent a little towards his MS but not reading, considering, listening, waiting to reply, intensely alive but quiet. 'What astonishing beauty' I thought looking at the austere modeling in the flat bright side lights from the train window. I do not think I talked much but he was becoming a real person to me.[33]

It was a conversation in which things seemed, as they sometimes do, "to take hold"; much followed from that afternoon's encounter: not one, but two Post-Impressionist exhibitions, a passionate affair, and a deep change in the artistic lives of these three principals, which in turn affected the whole Bloomsbury circle then taking shape. "After four years of wedded life and two children," Quentin Bell wrote, recollecting his mother's account, "there came that happy time when, as she put it, 'we stopped talking about "the good" and started talking about Cézanne'."[34]

For many years dismayed by contemporary English art, Fry had retreated into study of the Italian masters, and his first real seeing of Cézanne in 1906 had shocked him into attention: "The sky and the reflections in the pool are rendered as never before in landscape art, with an absolute illusion of the planes of illumination. The sky recedes miraculously behind the hillside, answered by the inverted concavity of lighted air in the pool."[35] Both Vanessa Bell and

Virginia Woolf were fond of remarking that no one had a greater sensitivity to landscape – its shapes and moods, its geometric and meteorological satisfactions – than did Roger Fry. Something of the natural, almost topological, quality of Fry's perception is conveyed in a well-known passage from Woolf's biography of Fry, where she situates him among the pictures he had assembled to be shown, now in the late fall of 1910, at the Grafton Gallery:

> And there was Roger Fry, gazing at them, plunging his eyes into them as if he were a hummingbird hawk-moth hanging over a flower, quivering yet still. And then drawing a deep breath of satisfaction, he would turn to whoever it might be, eager for sympathy. Were you puzzled? But why? And he would explain that it was quite easy to make the transition from Watts to Picasso; there was no break, only a continuation . He demonstrated; he persuaded; he argued. The argument rose and soared. It vanished into the clouds. Then back it swooped to the picture. So he talked in that gay crowded room, absorbed in what he was saying, quite unconscious of the impression he was making; fantastic yet reasonable, gentle yet fanatically obstinate, intolerant yet absolutely open-minded, and burning with the conviction that something very important was happening.[36]

The exhibit, "Manet and the Post-Impressionists" (christened in a moment of irritation when Roger Fry was talking to a reporter – he tried "expressionist" first, but the reporter didn't like that), opened in November. Fry had pressed Clive Bell and Desmond MacCarthy into service, and the three men had met in Paris to pick out the paintings they wanted. At that time, it was not difficult to borrow 21 Cézannes, 22 Van Goghs, and 35 Gauguins, along with an assortment of Manets and a Matisse; "nearly all those which Roger preferred were at our disposal,"[37] MacCarthy later recalled. The whole endeavor was in a Bloomsburyian spirit of high jinks and improvisation. Virginia Woolf describes, possibly apocryphally, the harum-scarum completion of the catalogue: "Desmond MacCarthy, pulled from his sickbed, given a bottle of champagne, and made to believe that his real job in life was art criticism, had written an introduction."[38]

They were all a bit taken aback by the fury with which the exhibit was received. Thirty years later Woolf devoted a vivid chapter to the two-year period of the exhibits, and reading her Fry biography now, one feels how deeply she absorbed from her sister and Duncan Grant and Fry the ways the exhibit affected their seeing. "The public in 1910," she wrote, "was thrown into paroxysms of rage and laughter,"[39] but what mattered to Fry "was that the young English artists were as enthusiastic about the works of Cézanne, Matisse and Picasso as he was. The first Post-Impressionist Exhibition, as many of them have testified, was to them a revelation; it was to affect their work profoundly."[40] Woolf continued to take an impudent pleasure in remembering how newspapers circulated caricatures of Fry and how the *Times'* reviewer proclaimed that the exhibited works constituted "the rejection of all that civilisation has done, the good with the bad."[41] The Bloomsburyites were acutely aware that the argument over paintings was also an argument over other things. In *Howard's End,* published that same year, E. M. Forster had made a careful study of forces similar to those at work at the reception of the exhibition: a sort of retrenching conservatism among the merchant classes faced as they were with the simultaneous triple uproar of women's liberation, worker agitation, and the threat of German armament. The French artists were reviled for the felt political offense in their bold coloration, dark outlines, spatial distortions. Fry found that his repeated pronouncements about movement in space fell on deaf ears among the audiences previously eager for his tony lectures on Tang china and Italian Renaissance masterworks. The exhibit furthered separations between him and the establishment and pushed him more definitely into the welcoming parlor of the Bells' house at 46 Gordon Square.

Roger Fry's affair with Vanessa Bell began the following year in 1911, after a trip to Turkey during which she suffered a miscarriage and Fry, with a combination of spiritual confidence, physical tirelessness, and a charming propensity for collecting up odd trouvailles and carting them back to the sickroom, nursed her back to health. The affair (which she eventually left for the universally appealing and largely homosexual Duncan Grant) lasted some three years, and if it changed Clive Bell's initial estimation of Fry he left very little evidence of it, though part of being a Post-Impressionist was understanding that all that mattered was honesty of relations. Open and complex form was always to be preferred over stodgy content, and Bloomsbury took a kind of pride in the convolution of its domestic affairs. Bell himself had had a long, unconsummated flirtation with Virginia Stephen, before she became Woolf, and, though he was now engaged in various pursuits of his own, none of these evolutions broke the strong strands of companionship he felt for Vanessa Bell. All the self-chroniclers of Bloomsbury – in the essays they wrote for the Memoir Club that they began together in the 1920s and kept going well into the 1960s – remark that it was a gift of Vanessa Bell's to hold happily together the most disparate personalities, to make for them a home to which they would always return. She loved to paint alongside her lovers; all the Bloomsbury abodes are much be-muraled – at Charleston even the bathtub is roseate. Quentin Bell has a particularly nice description of his mother's camaraderie with Duncan Grant, how "one felt a peculiarly happy intimacy when they were working side by side... There is," he continued, "a particular and indescribable charm about the relationship of two people united by love and friendship who work together in the same studio; for Vanessa it was I believe a most valuable experience."

Painting flowed easily into design, woodcuts, book jackets, furniture, ceramics, mosaics, all the projects of the Omega Workshops which had been started by Fry, with Vanessa Bell and Duncan Grant as co-directors. The workshop was intended, as Spalding writes, "to provide young artists with the opportunity to earn some money and to allow the influence of Post-Impressionism to invigorate decoration." Vanessa Bell's talents for design are on display here in the cases of visual work and of materials from the Hogarth Press. In many of them it is easy to discern the influence of Matisse and Derain as well as the Post-Impressionist affection for "primitives," from indigenous African art to those they called Italian primitives. Bell's own painting is very fine – her distinctive use of outlining black, which Roger Fry called her "slithery handwriting," sometimes gives the sense, well expressed by Spalding, "that she was discovering the forms and shapes as she drew."[42]

The second Post-Impressionist exhibit, in the fall of 1912, again at the Grafton Gallery, was conceived with a view toward continuing the enlightenment of the obdurate classes, and was, depending on whom you asked, a terrific success or a dire failure. This time the focus was more on Matisse and Picasso, with works by young French, Russian, and English painters, including Vanessa Bell and Duncan Grant (Grant's own style had changed radically since he had seen the first exhibit two years before). Again there was cacophony; again Roger Fry stood among the paintings with galvanism and indefatigability. Fry had in these years developed a roughly consistent language for discussing the work, and some of his thoughts and phrases were taken up, and probably slightly over-consolidated, in a book by Clive Bell, called *Art*, published in 1914, in which he usefully introduced the term (quite close to a phrase used by Fry) "significant form." Some years later, in an essay called "Retrospect," Fry looked back at the two Post-Impressionist exhibits and said something of the gratitude he felt on first coming upon Cézanne: "I gradually recognized that what I had hoped for as a possible event of some future century had already occurred, that art had begun to recover once more the language of design and to explore its so long neglected possibilities."[43] The best stewards of revolutions are able to articulate not only breaches but continuities, and this, too, was part of why that interpretation of Post-Impressionism arrived at and practiced by Fry, the Bells, Grant, and the Woolfs had such an impact on the English-speaking world.

Leonard Woolf, who was the secretary of the second exhibit as Clive Bell was secretary of the first, told a lovely story of going with Fry and Henry James about the exhibition rooms, winding up in the basement, "where," as Virginia Woolf added in, "among the packing cases and the brown paper, tea would be provided." According to Leonard Woolf, James expressed "in convoluted sentences the disturbed hesitations which Matisse and Picasso aroused in him, and Roger Fry, exquisitely, with something of the old-world courtesy which James carried with him," patiently countered. Virginia Woolf now takes the story in her own hands. Fry, she said, did "his best to convey to the great novelist what he meant by saying that Cézanne and Flaubert were, in a manner of speaking, after the same thing."[44]

Long after the exhibits and affairs were over, in the time of the enduring friendships, one further beautiful thing came from those initial sparks of Post-Impressionist fervor: Fry's small book on Cézanne, a long essay, really, of 80 pages, published in 1927 and still one of the very greatest essays ever written on Cézanne. Fry has here found inventions in prose that correspond to Cézanne's in paint – so that the sentences angle and crash up against each other, force the reader into private reconciliations, and eventually drop backward into depths of insight. Virginia Woolf admired this work above all: "the Cézanne stands out among Roger Fry's books like Mont Sainte-Victoire, solid in structure and bathed in light."[45]

Fry died in 1934; Woolf published her much-labored-over biography of him in 1939; she died in 1941; in 1943, Vanessa Bell sketched a group portrait of their Memoir Club. Like a miniature mural, like the diary entry that seeds the novel, this little picture has a whole world in outline. Among the depicted are Duncan Grant, Leonard Woolf, Clive and Vanessa Bell, Desmond MacCarthy, Quentin Bell, and E. M. Forster, while from the wall look down the absent spirits: Lytton Strachey, Virginia Woolf, and Roger Fry. One can't help but feel that Fry is everywhere present – aren't all these lines caught up with his ideas of rhythm, form, and space; isn't the painting's own memoir, its own significant memory, the great bursting open of those French exhibits, now 30 years in the past? From the point of view of the public, the scheme had, as Clive Bell had seen right away, been fantastic. But the exhibit also brought the Bloomsbury figures into new arrangements and relations, and made a lasting landscape for their lived endeavors. It was Vanessa Bell who had seen these deeper possibilities: "'what astonishing beauty' . . . I do not think I talked much, but he was becoming a real person to me."

38. Roger Fry, *Original Woodcuts by Various Artists*
London: Omega Workshops Ltd., 1918
Private collection

First edition, limited to 75 hand-numbered copies (this is copy #49) printed for the Omega Workshops by Richard Madley, London. Each full-page woodcut printed heavily in black faces a page with its title. Pictured above is Vanessa's "Nude." Other contributions include:

Fry: Still Life
Gertler (drawn) and Fry (woodcut): Harlequinade
Bell: Dahlias
Grant: The Hat Shop
Fry: The Cup
Simon Bussy: Black Cat
Fry: The Stocking
Roald Kristian: Animals
Edward Wolfe: Ballet
Grant: The Tub
Edward McKnight Kauffer: Study; sharing a page with Edward Wolfe: Group.

Roger Fry founded the Omega Workshops in 1913 as a collective, to provide a source of income for young artists. Under the sponsorship of Roger, with Vanessa and Duncan as co-directors, they and others worked no more than two or three days a week to provide decorative articles for sale to support their individual artistic endeavors, to which they devoted their remaining days and hours. Omega was Roger's passion, and he was bitterly disillusioned when it failed as a business in 1919.

39. Roger Fry, *Vanessa Bell*
Ca. 1917
The Henry W. and Albert A. Berg Collection of English and American Literature, Astor Lenox and Tilden Foundations, The New York Public Library

Roger Fry shot many photographs of Vanessa; this one dates, likely, to the late nineteen-teens or early 'twenties, after their affair had spent itself. Their affair, however, validated Vanessa's liberation from the nineteenth century mores of her parents and established the foundation of a lifelong intimacy with Roger. Though they shared aesthetic and physical passions, Vanessa left Roger for Duncan, and the three of them led one of Bloomsbury's most openly puzzling relationships.

40. *Vanessa Bell*

Ca. 1881

Mortimer Rare Book Room, Smith College

Baby Vanessa, in a pose that prefigures her modeling for Roger Fry, is captured here at about age two or three.

41. Vanessa Bell, On Being Ill

Preliminary sketch in pencil, ink, and watercolor
Ca. 1930
Private collection

Virginia Woolf, On Being Ill

Printed and published by Leonard & Virginia Woolf at the Hogarth Press, 1930
Private collection

Bell's preliminary design for the 1930 limited edition publication of Virginia's essay. Scribbled notes on the Bell family social schedule are visible on the left-hand border of the sketch. With a first edition of this essay not published separately in the United States; limited to 250 copies numbered and signed by Woolf (in purple ink), who set the type.

John Lehmann, in his memoir *Thrown to the Woolfs*, illuminates Virginia and Vanessa's collaborative roles in designing her dust-jackets: "Vanessa's jackets have come to be thought of as an integral part of Virginia's books, the perfect sisterly accord of writer and artist sharing the same vision. In fact the truth was rather different." In 1931 Vanessa wrote to Lehmann, "I've not read a word of the book [*The Waves*] – I only have had the vaguest description of it and of what she wants me to do from Virginia – but that has always been the case with the jackets I have done for her."[46]

Vanessa is indeed correct in asserting that the relationship of her designs to her sister's texts is at best minimal, but inasmuch as her style grew to embody the Bloomsbury aesthetic, her jackets are the ideal public faces to Woolf's books.

This is the last of Woolf's hand-printed books. Rhein calls it "one of the showpieces in the private press tradition...." She notes,

> What distinguished *On Being Ill* and the books which follow it is a feel and sensitivity which are immediately discernible to sight and touch ... [and] which are out of character for the Woolfs and contrary to their original aesthetic concepts. On Being Ill looks as if it had been designed as a smart commercial publication or at least as an attempt to emulate such a style by hand ... though it might be argued that this book reflected the newly found wealth and social position which came to Virginia after her best selling decade of the 1920s, the concept and execution seem rather to indicate the interests and influences of the younger men and women who had come to the Press with hopes of learning the fine art of printing, inspired by the heroic feats of contemporaries.[47]

On Being Ill was previously printed in the *New Criterion*, January 1926; reprinted in *Forum*, April 1926, under the title "Illness: An Unexplored Mine"; and reprinted in *The Moment and Other Essays* and in *Collected Essays Volume 4*, with its final title. Woolf revised the text slightly for this limited edition, and retained those changes in subsequent publications (Kirkpatrick A14, noting that the Woolfs had originally planned an edition of 125 copies, but because the edition was oversubscribed, they doubled that figure. At that point the copies that had already been printed were altered so that "125" at the colophon was crossed out and replaced by "250," with the balance bound with a freshly printed colophon leaf. Kirkpatrick proposes that about 25 likely jacketless copies – but possibly more – were distributed free, with the altered colophon.)

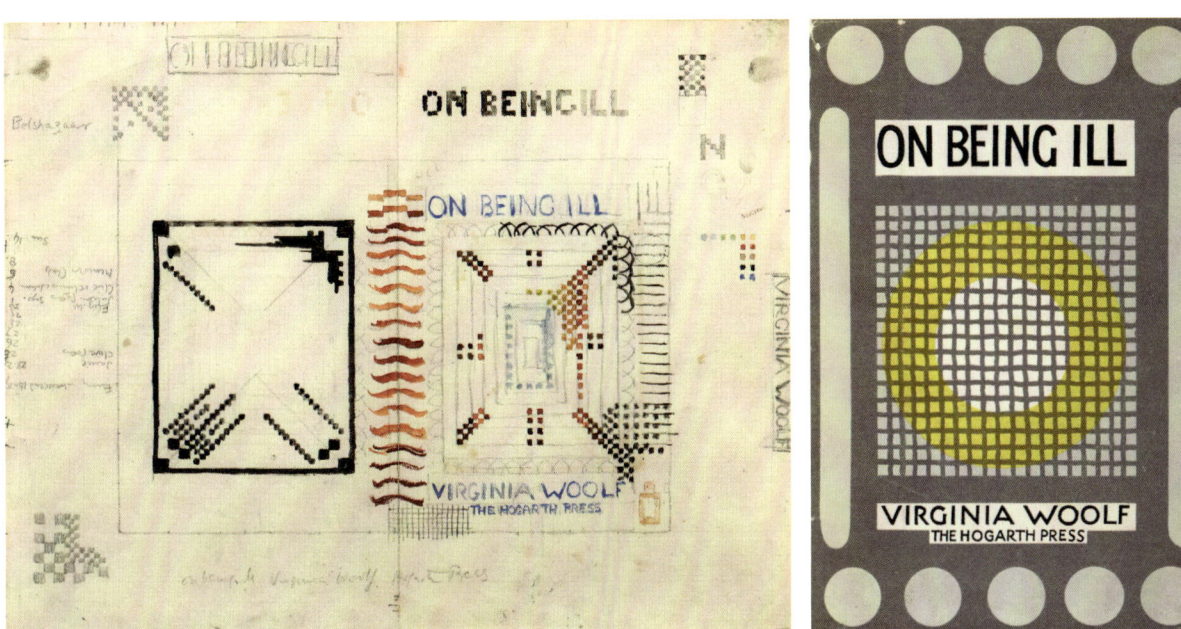

In "On Being Ill" Virginia wonders why "illness has not taken its place with love and battle and jealousy among the prime themes of literature." With few exceptions, she points out, "literature does its best to maintain that its concern is with the mind; that the body is a sheet of plain glass through which the soul looks straight and clear, and, save for one or two passions such as desire and greed, is null, and negligible and non-existent. On the contrary, the very opposite is true. All day, all night the body intervenes; blunts or sharpens, colours or discolours ." She attributes this disparity to every writer's fear that readers will criticize a lack of "plot" and "the poverty of the language": "English, which can express the thoughts of Hamlet and the tragedy of Lear, has no words for the shiver and the headache."

42. Virginia Woolf, Foreword, *Recent Paintings by Vanessa Bell*

The London Artists' Association
February 4 to March 8, 1930
Private collection

Virginia Woolf, Foreword, *Catalogue of Recent Paintings by Vanessa Bell*

Alex. Reid & Lefevre, Ltd. (The Lefevre Galleries)
London: March 1934
Private collection

First appearance of this short essay by Woolf on her sister's work, in a catalogue for Vanessa's exhibition in the spring of 1930 at The Cooling Galleries (92 New Bond Street) courtesy of the London Artists' Association – "sole agents," as they note on the lower panel, for the works of Bell, Fry, Grant, and eleven others. Maynard Keynes is listed among the four guarantors of the Association. Following Virginia's four-page foreword, 27 pieces are listed, ranging in price from 25 to 50 guineas. Five hundred copies of this fragile pamphlet were printed by the Favil Press and likely distributed gratis (Kirkpatrick B10).

She begins her foreword with insight, and humor, on the contemporary art market and on her sister's work. She claims that it is unusual for a female artist to have a solo show: art means nudity, and "it was held, until sixty years ago that for a woman to look upon nakedness with the eye of an artist, and not simply with the eye of mother, wife or mistress was corruptive of her innocency and destructive of her domesticity. Hence the extreme activity of women in philanthropy, society, religion and all pursuits requiring clothing" (1). The balance of her essay is devoted to the question of the language of an art object, the story it tells, or doesn't. She sees "serene yet temperate warmth" in her sister's work, the creation, time and again, of a "serene and ordered world." And yet these paintings do not present narratives. "No stories are told; no insinuations are made" (2).

"Mrs. Bell has a certain reputation it cannot be denied" (1), and one might hope, she posits, to learn something of Vanessa by examining her art. There, too, the viewer is thwarted:

> Her pictures do not betray her. Their reticence is inviolable. That is why they intrigue and draw us on; that is why, if it be true that they yield their full meaning only to those who can tunnel their way behind the canvas into masses and passages and relations and values of which we know nothing – if it be true that she is a painter's painter – still her pictures claim us and make us stop. They give us an emotion. They offer a puzzle. And the puzzle is that while Mrs. Bell's pictures are immensely expressive, their expressiveness has no truck with words (3).

The catalogue for the 1934 exhibit of Vanessa's work at the Lefevre Galleries in London includes a foreword by Virginia; this time her single page of text is followed by a list of 36 paintings – including portraits of Virginia, of "Mrs. Grant," and of Roger Fry – with items 37-48 collectively listed as "original designs for plates." Virginia opens this essay by invoking Keats, to let us know that no traditional art criticism awaits: "I have ever been too sensible," he wrote to Haydon, "of the labyrinthian path to eminence in Art to think I understand the emphasis of Painting." What follows is a breathless, wordy portrait of the gallery of art, saying more about the viewers than the viewed:

Nobody moves and yet the room is full of intimate relationships. People's minds have split out of their bodies and become part of their surroundings . Character is colour, and colour is china, and china is music . Everywhere life has been rid of its accidents, shown in its essence. The weight of custom has been lifted from the earth . In short, precipitated by the swift strokes of the painter's brush, we have been blown over the boundary to the world where words talk such nonsense that it is best to silence them. And it is a world of glowing serenity and sober truth. Compare it, for example, with Piccadilly Circus or St. James's Square.

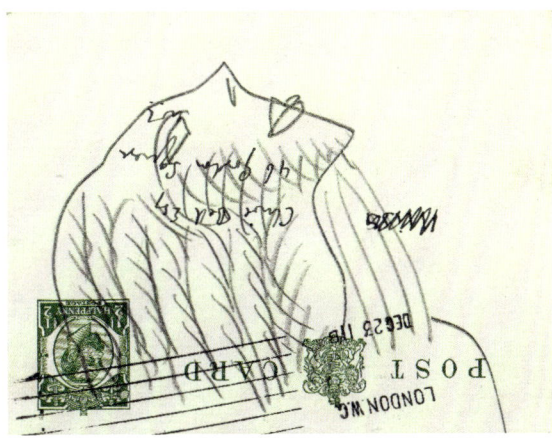 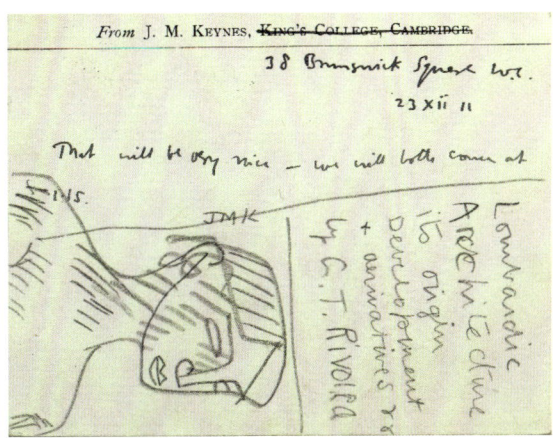

43. Duncan Grant, *Postcard sketches*

1911

Private collection

Two sketches – one per side – drafted on a postcard bearing an innocuous note from Maynard Keynes (who has altered by hand the printed address on his card from King's College, Cambridge, to 38 Brunswick Sq.) to Clive Bell at 46 Gordon Square, and postmarked December 23, 1911 – "That will be very nice – we will both come at 1:15." It seems likely that Duncan, also living at this time at Gordon Square, picked up this postcard as he would have a bit of scrap paper to sketch quickly these figures in keeping with one of his most important works, *Head of Eve*, painted in oil in 1913 and now residing at the Tate Collection. Their description of this work, but for their mention of color, could easily apply to the strong busts pictured on this card: "Grant liked to fuse many different stylistic influences in his work, and he was particularly interested in the invigorating example of non-Western art forms. The mask-like face and symmetrical pose of Head of Eve suggest a sensual Eden by drawing on Byzantine mosaics as well as the wooden masks of the African Fang tribe. The simplified form and intense colour lend a sense of commanding immediacy."

With an additional note in Duncan's hand referring to the voluminous and copiously illustrated two-volume work translated by G. McN. Rushforth and published by William Heinemann in 1910: *Lombardic Architecture: Its Origin, Development, and Derivatives by G.T. Rivola*. A copy of this two-volume work is in Clive Bell's study at Charleston.

44. Lytton Strachey, *Autograph letter signed to Duncan Grant*

May 19, 1918
Private collection

Lytton writes with concern that Duncan is jeopardizing his conscientious objector status by entertaining the notion of becoming an official painter:

> I am feeling slightly alarmed by the news that you think of becoming an official painter. Doesn't it put your position as a C.O. in some danger? I suppose it certainly comes under the heading of "propaganda" work: and it seems to me that that is just the sort of excuse people in authority might use if they wanted to be nasty at some future time. If Beaverbrook supports you, no doubt you're safe – but how long will Beaverbrook be where he is? Also, to judge from his doings with poor Mr. [Grein], His Lordship is anyhow not very trustworthy. Apart from this (which I think is the most serious part of the business), I don't believe you would find it at all agreeable working for such persons, and I'm sure that whatever you did you would never satisfy them, and that it would be very difficult to avoid all sorts of unpleasantnesses. There is also the question of the respectability of the job – which does strike me as rather dubious. It seems a pity, after having kept clear of this [] for so long, to begin to have truck with it.
>
> The main advantage would I suppose be that you escape from your present servitude; but perhaps you would only be exchanging it for a worse one.

Duncan's financial instability proved inspirational to Roger Fry who, in 1913, founded the Omega Workshops in the hope of providing part-time decorative jobs to help sustain artists in their more serious pursuits. By 1918, however, it was near folding, and Duncan and others had a hard time making ends meet. Duncan considered, as a last resort, taking a government post. All of Bloomsbury, though, objected to the war, some more formally than others, and it is this of which Lytton reminds him. Clive, Duncan, Lytton, Adrian, and others publicly opposed conscription. Leonard and Lytton were excused on medical grounds. The others sought refuge through farm work – Vanessa and Duncan moved to Charleston in 1916 toward this very end, and Ottoline Morrell hosted many friends on the farm at Garsington. Virginia, writing in her 1938 memoir of Julian, just after his death in the Spanish Civil War, had this to say about the younger generation's participation in international conflicts: "I have never known anyone of my generation [to] have that feeling about a war. We were all CO's in the Great War. And though I understand that this is a 'cause,' can be called the cause of liberty and so on, still my natural reaction is to fight intellectually: The moment force is used, it becomes meaningless and unreal to me."

45. Duncan Grant, *Autograph postcard signed to Vanessa Bell*

Postmarked June 4, 1927
Private collection

Writing from Paris in 1927, Duncan thanks her for her letter, sends news of mutual friends, and describes his recent visit to de Beaumont's Soirées de Paris, where he saw Diaghilev's Ballets Russes perform Erik Satie's *Mercure*, choreographed by Léonide Massine, who also performed:

> I went to a cheap seat at the ballet & saw Picasso's new ballet Mercure. Very interesting. Massine danced in it. However you will see it in London. I also saw Picasso who was so sorry to miss you & and asked me to go & see him which I may do tomorrow.

Picasso designed the sets – as he had for work with Satie and Massine in the past, most notably for *Parade* in 1917. In fact, *Mercure* might be the best work he had done since *Parade*:

> Although formalistically Picasso's designs for the latter part of his first theatrical phase are sometimes in the same vein as *Parade*, in that they are frequently composed of a number of juxtaposed disparate elements, they never achieve the same level of innovation and creativity. *Mercure*, as yet largely unexamined, may well in terms of innovation prove to be the successor to *Parade*. Essentially experimental, and revolving around a succession of episodes which depicted aspects of the personality of the god Mercury, it was composed of a series of *poses plastiques*. Picasso's designs, which included movable scenery that was manipulated by the dancers, created a furore – as had those for *Parade* – and, against the criticisms of the contemporary press, he was supported by leading avant garde artists and critics of the day, including Georges Auric, André Breton, and Max Ernst.[48]

Vanessa, with Roger, Clive, and Molly MacCarthy, had been taken by Gertrude Stein to meet Picasso in his studio in January 1914, and she was as profoundly impressed by the man as she had been by his art. Duncan shortly thereafter visited Picasso's studio with the formidable Miss Stein and was similarly affected. Thereafter, both followed Picasso's achievements, but Duncan's art showed more evidence of the master's influence than did Vanessa's.

46. Dora Carrington – Frances Marshall (later Partridge), *Correspondence*

Ca. 1924-1926
Private collection

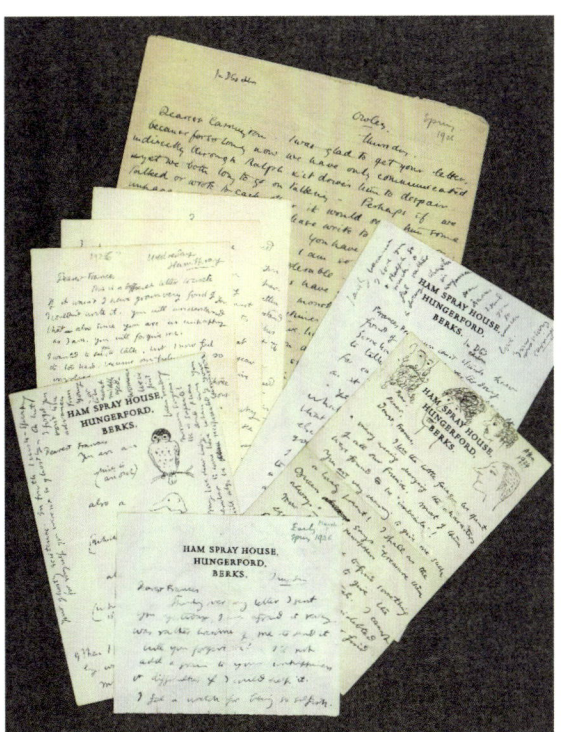

A series of letters in which Slade artist Carrington and Frances Marshall negotiate for the time and affection of Ralph Partridge. The relationship among Carrington, her idol Lytton Strachey, her husband Ralph Partridge – coincidentally, the first paid assistant at the Hogarth Press and far from their most beloved – and his lover Frances Marshall makes the Bell-Grant household seem comparatively conventional. Carrington, in love with the confirmed homosexual Lytton, moved in with him at Ham Spray House in 1917. She married Ralph, deeply in love with her, in 1921, and the two lived together with Lytton, from 1922. Despite her love for Lytton and her commitment to her husband, Carrington had an affair with Ralph's close friend Gerald Brennan. Ralph followed suit, initiating a liason with considerably more staying power with Frances. Lytton, meanwhile, was in love with Ralph, and threatened to leave Carrington if she lost her husband. Ralph began in 1923 spending weekdays with Frances in London and weekends at Ham Spray with Carrington and Lytton.

The letters present here, all composed between 1924 and 1926, show Carrington desperately trying to pry her husband from the grasp of Frances – to whom she felt close and whom she had even, in the past, propositioned. Frances's response is also present. In an undated letter composed at Ham Spray, Carrington sends amusing sketches, thanks her for a gift, propositions her good-naturedly, and writes in the hope of a visit that weekend if it rains:

> I still maintain if that vulture [i.e., Ralph?] wasn't so devouring, I should very quickly gain your attentions Miss, to say nothing of your bed – If it is fine think kindly of me. If it is wet I shall see you here, & show you, I hope, my affection. You say you like me more than I like you —? How can we prove such a delicate point? Ralph returned looking rather hollow-eyed, & worn but very gay and happy – for which I am to thank —? Remember always that there are few people fonder of you than your Carrington.

In another letter, also undated but clearly later, she writes from Ham Spray in desperation; Ralph seems to have decided to leave her for Frances, and Carrington, contemplating the loss then of both her husband and of her Lytton, offers terms of a "treaty":

> We each know what we have all three been feeling these last months – now it is more or less over. The treaty has to be drawn up. I have to face that owing to a situation, which cannot be got over, I must give up living with R. I simply now write quite frankly, to beg you to try, while these adjustments are being made, to see the position from my point of view & to try & see, if is not [in?]compatible with your happiness, to still let me keep some of my friendship with R.
>
> I do love R., only in a different way, just as you love him. It isn't any easier for me to give him up than it would be for you. The bare truth from my point of view is that <u>if</u> R. leaves me completely, or to all practical purposes completely, it really means an end of this life. Even although the happiness of my relation with Lytton, ironically, is so bound up with R., that that will be wrecked.
>
> I am <u>obliged</u> to accept this situation. You must see that. All I can do is to beg you to be, any rate at first, a little generous. You see I've no pride, I write a letter which I suppose I oughtn't to write.
>
> You see, Frances, you can afford to be lenient because R. is so completely yours in his affections. In spite of all your difficulties, & unhappiness, you are a gainer, we losers. And if you face it, the sitation really is <u>that R can only give me what you can spare to give.</u> My future does rest with you.
>
> Because I regard it all beyond us, in an odd way. I send you my love. I hope you are happier. Forgive me if I should not have written perhaps however you will understand. It would be kind if you burnt this letter, for it was rather difficult to write.
>
> I send my love to you, Yr Carrington.
>
> Reading this over, I see I've expressed it very badly. And probably it's pointless – But I feel

rather in despair so forgive me & don't pay any attention to it if you don't want to. There seems to be no answer, but perhaps you will write.

She writes again immediately the next day: "Please forgive me for writing yesterday. It was really the outcome of a very strong desire I've had for many weeks to talk to you. My fondest love, Carrington. And don't answer my letter. Because there is nothing to say. I see that now." Frances, however, does respond, in a three-page communication of support:

> You have always been such an angel to me and I am so fond of you that it makes it all the more intolerable – this horrible knot in which our happinesses have got involved.
>
> I know that I must seem a monster to you. I want just to explain how though sometimes in black moments you become an entity & I have horrid feelings about you, always when I think of you as yourself I feel nothing but fondness for you. And I'm sure I am often to you an abstract monster. I explain it so badly.
>
> I never never never feel that if R. should live with me I should want him not to see you very often & go on being fond of you . I know how difficult it is to go on seeing people on the same terms when the circumstances have changed, and he seemed afraid that you might feel you couldn't bear to see him at all. Do believe that that is the most awful thought imaginable to me as well as to him . I raised objections to the half-&-half life theory proposed by Lytton in our conversation. I objected to that because it didn't seem to me a solution but simply a continuation of the present situation, that the strain on everyone's nerves would be as great if not greater than before, that particularly for R. it would be intolerable – & that it really is necessary (for practical reasons such as work incidentally as well) to have roots in one place and not two.
>
> Because I love R. & want to live with him, & want him to share my life instead of being a visitor into it, I can't see how I could find this incompatible with his being fond of you & seeing you every day of his life . One of the saddest results of this situation is the difficulties it puts between you & me. I send you my love if you feel you can bear a monster's love.

47. Virginia Woolf, *Night and Day*
London: Duckworth and Company, 1919
Private collection

First edition; dedicated to Vanessa, who was the jumping off point for the protagonist, Katherine Hilberry: "To Vanessa Bell / But, looking for a phrase, I found none to stand beside your name"; 2,000 copies. A second printing, of 1,000 copies, was issued in 1920. In February 1929 Duckworth sold the rights to the Hogarth Press (Kirkpatrick A4a).

A gift copy, inscribed on the front endpaper by Lytton Strachey to Dora Carrington – *D.C. from L.S.* – and further signed, *Frances Partridge.*

Lytton purchased this copy for Carrington as soon as it was published, and both read it immediately. Lytton wrote a letter of admiration to Virginia who responded, "I don't suppose there's anything in the way of praise that means more to me than yours." He then wrote to Ottoline Morrell and described the book as "a work not to read, but to re-read." Carrington sent Gerald Brenan a letter advising him to read it. The book became a cherished addition to the Strachey–Carrington Library. After Lytton's death in 1932, Carrington took her own life. Her husband Ralph, who had inherited many of their effects including a substantial part of the library, then married Frances, who likely signed this copy either during their marriage or after Ralph's death in 1960.

Most of Virginia's friends labeled *Night and Day*, her most conventional novel in form and subject, a failure, and eventually she concurred. Some recent critics have promoted it as an expert parody, and at least one as a response to Leonard's *The Wise Virgins* (1914), but such assessments, if kind, are aberrant. Though a well-executed example of its genre, it is little more than a novel of manners that follows the romantic entanglements of its ensemble cast. The story has it origins in the early life of Vanessa. In 1919, Virginia explained the book to her former tutor, Janet Case: "[T]ry to think of Katharine [Hilbery] as Vanessa, not me; and suppose her concealing a passion for painting and forced to go into society by George [Duckworth] – that was the beginning of her; *but* as one goes on, all sorts of things happen … and then there's the whole question, which interested me, again too much for the book's sake, I daresay, of things one doesn't say; what effect does that have?"

Having begun the novel in early 1915, Woolf was relieved and satisfied upon completion. Lytton wrote her a letter full of praise, and Clive called it "[n]o doubt a work of the highest genius," to which she responded with wary gratitude. She wrote in her diary, "I think I feel most doubtful about Morgan [Forster]; after getting his report I shall be quite at ease. Three or four people count, & the rest, save as a senseless clapping of hands or hissing, are nowhere. No one of much intelligence, outside my own friends, is likely to read a very long novel."

She had been right to be "doubtful": Forster wrote to her privately, "I like it less than the V.O.," and she recoiled: "Though he spoke also of great admiration, & had read in haste & proposed re-reading, this rubbed out all the pleasure of the rest ." In 1924, Clive offered his opinion publicly and less gently than before, calling it in *The Dial* "her most definite failure," with a theme "ill-chosen because it cramped and choked the natural deflagration of the artist's mind." Virginia herself eventually acknowledged a degree of truth to these evaluations. In 1925 she referred to its "flatness."[49] In 1930 she made excuses to Ethel Smyth: "After being ill and suffering every form and variety of nightmare and extravagant intensity of perception when I came to, I was so tremblingly afraid of my own insanity that I wrote *Night and Day* mainly to prove to my own satisfaction that I could keep entirely off that dangerous ground. Bad as the book is, it composed my mind, and I think taught me certain elements of composition which I should not have had the patience to learn had I been in full flush of health always."

In 1938, in response to Philip Morrell's compliments, she brushed it aside as "a book written in half hour laps in bed, and so tedious to remember, and, I have always been told, a complete failure to read. Nothing will make me read it: but owning to your letter, a faint sunset glow surrounds it on the shelf."

V. Books as Objects
The Hogarth Press and Beyond

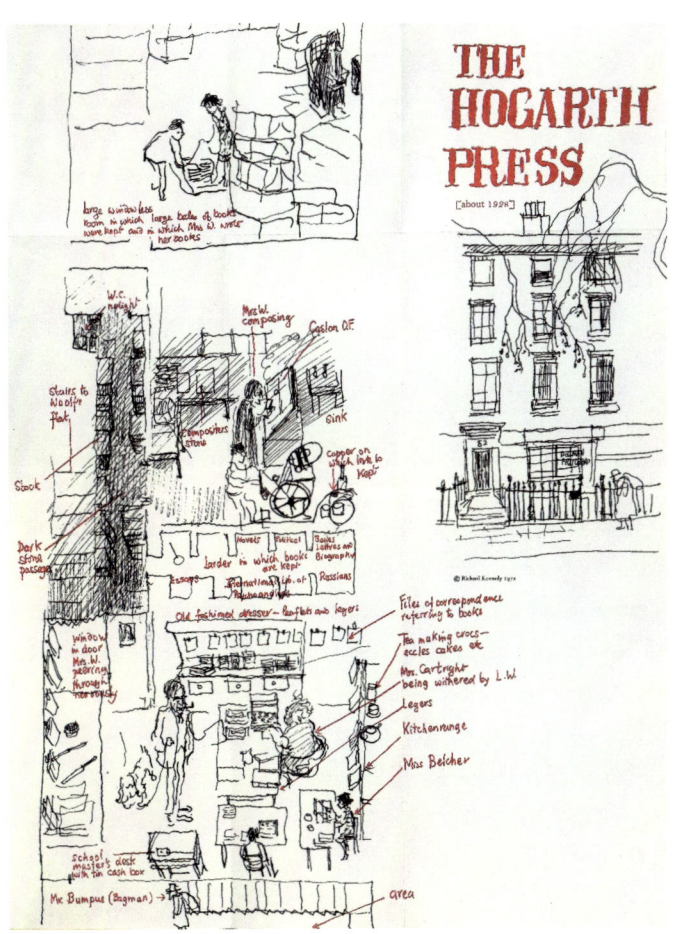

Richard Kennedy, *Map of the Hogarth Press*
London: Heinemann, 1972
Private collection

In Marriage, in Print, in Business   Sarah Funke

Virginia and Leonard purchased their first printing press in 1917, ostensibly as therapy for Virginia and as a way to publish short works of dubious commercial potential by themselves and their circle. The Hogarth Press soon evolved into a creative and political forum for the Bloomsbury Group, as they published the work of family, friends, and like-minded colleagues: independent works in all genres, as well as series designed by Leonard and Virginia. Eventually viewed as an organ for the Modernist movement in English literature, ultimately the Press became a symbol for the authorial control impossible to secure through larger firms. Over time, it would be a source of as much pride, joy, freedom, frustration, hope, aggravation, and expense to the couple as children would have been (although ultimately quite profitable).

Whether to have children was a question that plagued Virginia throughout her life. Leonard felt that her mental instability was prohibitive, and Virginia then invested her maternal instincts in the lives of her niece and nephews – Angelica, Julian, and Quentin. Meanwhile, Leonard sought a pursuit to keep her hands and mind busy at least, they planned, on a part-time basis. For over a decade Virginia had pursued her interest in bookbinding – with informal lessons, experimentation with different materials, and even the invention of a new method – and her cumulative knowledge and interest in the handicraft of books would spur her on at the Press.

They inaugurated their printing venture – a "hobby of printing rather than publishing" – with *Two Stories*: "Three Jews" by Leonard and "The Mark on the Wall" by Virginia, the pair illustrated by four woodcuts by Carrington. Virginia wrote enthusiastically to Vanessa: " there's nothing in writing compared with printing,"[50] and was so excited about the prospect of printing this book that she began production before writing her contribution. As novice printers, the Woolfs found the first venture taxing. There was two months of tedious, exacting typesetting, searching for inks and inking techniques that would result in a clean page, and then the ordeal of binding and distribution. In the end both Virginia and Leonard seemed pleased with the result, despite its imperfections: the woodcut on page 19 was printed at an angle; page 25 bears a typographical error ("country Housse"). At the beginning of May 1917 they announced the limited edition of *Two Stories* with a one-page notice of the edition of 150 copies and an order form mailed to friends and family. Immediately they sold 134 copies to 91 buyers – Roger Fry, for one, wanted multiple copies to sell through his Omega Workshops, to showcase the Omega paper used to cover some of the copies. (Their bind-as-needed process, however, resulted in at least three binding variants, not all papers coming from Omega.) With their stock nearly exhausted, they raised the price from 1s. 6d. to 2s. By 1922 it was fetching more than ten times its original price in second-hand bookshops. (Woolmer 1, Kirkpatrick A2a)

Their note at the top of the title page suggested it was the inaugural volume in a series: "Publication No. 1." Although the strict serial plan was dropped (though would later be revived in their series of individually published letters and essays), the fundamental concept of printing material written on assignment from the Press remained. An exception was occasionally made for the work of writers who, they felt, needed promotion and in the case of poetry that had enjoyed a previous appearance, for example T. S. Eliot's *The Waste Land* (1923). Contributors and readers alike readily put their faith in the Woolfs' abilities. Before Virginia had even begun "The Mark on the Wall" – a story Lytton would call "a work of genius" – she wrote to Vanessa: "We've got about 60 orders already which shows a trusting spirit."[51] With experience and exposure the Woolfs would develop from amateur printers to seasoned publishers, introducing the world to works by several important Modernist writers. Over time their aesthetic, first inspired by Roger Fry and his Omega Workshops, would become better planned and more expertly executed, but there was never mistaking a Hogarth Press title for the product of a more traditional house.

Donna E. Rhein, in her history of the Press, examines *Two Stories* in the context of their future productions. Though the Woolfs wrote enthusiastically to Carrington about the four woodcuts that appear here, ultimately they did not have the expertise necessary to reproduce artwork attractively; only eight of their next 33 publications bear illustrations. They would repeatedly employ capital letters on the cover and title page, as well as wide margins and generous leading – in contrast with the "close lines and closely spaced type popularized by William Morris" – perhaps in consideration of their readers who were "faced with poor inking and gray type." *Two Stories* is sewn into wrappers, but they would also try gluing and stapling before settling on a method combining gluing and sewing. The later books would, on the whole, be neater productions, reflecting not just better planning and the knowledge derived from experience, but a refined aesthetic.

Their second book was to be Katherine Mansfield's *Prelude*, but they interrupted typesetting to produce a memorial volume to Leonard's brother Cecil, recently killed in battle. That small, simple pamphlet is, hands-down, the black tulip of the hand-printed Hogarth Press titles. Works followed by their friends, with terms set at a percentage of the profits – though hefty portions of the small runs (which on two successful occasions grew as sales progressed) were often recycled. The pages they printed were haphazardly, if lovingly, bound as needed, with varied labels, in varied wrappers – provided by Roger Fry and his Omega Workshops, or by a source in Czechoslovakia, or acquired on various travels – effectively calling attention to their contents, at times controversially. Little was attempted by way of publicity, which was largely word of mouth through their complex and far-reaching grapevine. Up until 1923, sales were by subscription; after that, newspaper ads and printed publication announcements became more regular, gradually bringing about an end to the printing of a backlist at the conclusion of each text.

When their seventh publication, Woolf's own *Kew Gardens* (1919), sold out quickly enough to warrant a second printing, they took the opportunity to correct a rather serious problem with the first run, changing their colophon from "Leonard and Virginia" to "L. and V. Woolf." In 1921, on Leonard's 41st birthday, Woolf wrote in her diary of their need for additional staff: "the Hogarth Press, you see, begins to outgrow its parents."[52]

Authors ranged from the ungifted but related (socially or by blood) to others who are still remembered (and are in print), some of whom would become friends. Most notable among these is Eliot. In the summer of 1923 Virginia and Leonard finished setting type for their edition of *The Waste Land*, without question their poetry title with the longest shelf-life, by the friend who would become the most prestigious poet in their stable. (Freud was their most lucrative author and, arguably, their most famous over the long haul, however their relationship was not an intimate one with Freud, but a professional one with the PsychoAnalytical Institute.) Despite the fact that it was their 18th hand-printed book, it contained the usual flaws that marred their productions from first to last and that marked their books as the products of acute intelligence, if rather obtuse handicraft. Rhein writes, "As usual, the text of *The Waste Land* is not black enough for comfortable reading and there are some light places from uneven inking. Why the Woolfs made a habit of printing several label styles for an edition is a mystery when they knew by the time the labels were needed how many books were in the run."[53] At least when they came to prepare the backlist for this volume they "were considerate enough of the text not to place the advertisements opposite a printed page or on the verso of the last text page."[54]

With the completion of *The Waste Land* Virginia articulated how she felt about her work at the Press at that time, after a particularly challenging project: "we have finished Tom," she writes in her diary, "much to our relief. He will be published this August by Marjorie; & altogether we have worked at full speed since May. & that is I'm persuaded the root & source & origin of all health & happiness, provided of course that one rides work as a man rides a great horse, in a spirited & independent way; not a drudge, but a man with spurs in his heels."[55]

In 1924 the Woolfs embarked on a high-risk, high-reward venture whose financial importance to the Press is belied by Virginia's virtual silence on the subject. In taking on the first two volumes of Freud's *Collected Papers* at the end of that year, and becoming the official publisher of the papers of the International PsychoAnalytical Institute and the authorized publisher in English of his work, Leonard, at the instigation of Lytton's brother James, put the whole operation at risk of "prosecution for either blasphemy or obscenity."[56] And yet, beyond commenting in 1921 on the appearance of James and Alix Strachey, visiting from Vienna where they were studying with Freud, Virginia writes just this, in 1924: "Dadie came back yesterday & we had a jolly afternoon doing up Freud."[57] And then? Nothing, for over a decade. It was only after she met the man – "an old fire now flickering"[58] – in 1939 that she mentions him again, and only after his death, it seems, that she began to read his works.[59] Nevertheless, throughout the 1920s and '30s their Freud concession was responsible for a substantial percentage of their publishing income.

In 1938, Virginia sold her share in the Press to former assistant John Lehmann, but as Leonard wrote in his autobiography, the "development of the Hogarth Press was bound up with the development of Virginia as a writer and with her literary or creative psychology,"[60] and today "the Hogarth Press" is synonymous with "Virginia Woolf." Virginia herself wrote in her journal in 1925: "How my handwriting goes downhill! Another sacrifice to the Hogarth Press, yet what I owe the Hogarth Press is barely paid by the whole of my handwriting . yes, I'm the only woman in England free to write what I like."[61] As other Bloomsbury children outlived their parents, the Hogarth Press continued after Virginia sold her share in it, and it even survived her death, and Leonard's too, becoming an affiliate of Chatto & Windus in 1946.

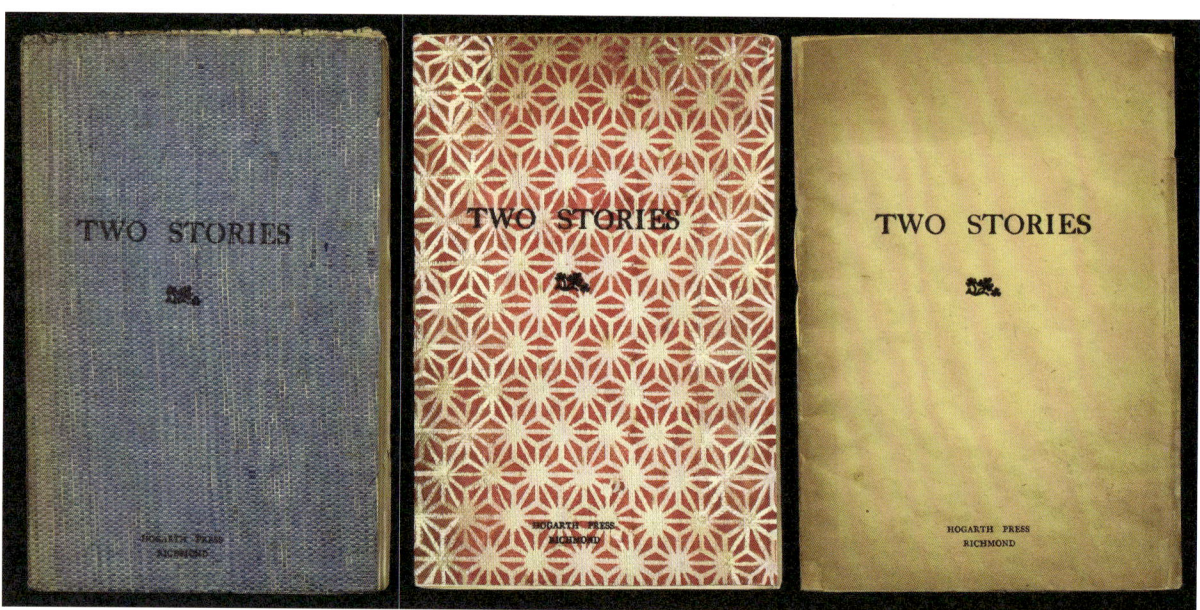

48. Leonard Woolf / Virginia Woolf, *Two Stories*
Richmond: The Hogarth Press, 1917
Private collection

Blue cloth wrappers, stamped in black; with an autograph letter from Virginia to Bunny Garnett loosely inserted, and with Bunny's bookplate to the title page.

Leonard Woolf / Virginia Woolf, *Two Stories*
Richmond: The Hogarth Press, 1917
Private collection

Red and white cloth wrappers, stamped in black.

Leonard Woolf / Virginia Woolf, *Two Stories*
Richmond: The Hogarth Press, 1917
Private collection

Yellow paper wrappers, printed in black.

The Hogarth Press, *Printed announcement for subscribers*
Ca. 1919
Private collection

Leonard Woolf, *Typed letter signed to John Mavrogordato*
June 20, 1918
One leaf of Hogarth House stationery
Private collection

Three copies of the first edition of the Woolfs' first publication, a joint booklet including "Three Jews" by Leonard and "The Mark on the Wall" by Virginia. Each in variant wrappers.

Together with a printed announcement alerting potential subscribers to the works of the Hogarth Press:

> Dear Sir, Our object in starting the Hogarth Press has been to publish at low prices short works of merit, in prose or poetry, which could not, because of their merits, appeal to a very large public. The whole process of printing and production (except in one instance) is done by ourselves, and the editions are necessarily extremely small, not exceeding 300 copies. We enclose a list of publications with an order form.

They go on to suggest a subscription plan in which deposits are received – "For the convenience of those who might desire to purchase copies and to avoid the necessity of continually sending small sums of money." By the end of 1919, the Woolfs had published eight small books, one of which, due to its size (their sixth: J. Middleton Murry's *The Critic in Judgment*), was hand-printed by the Prompt Press but bound by the Woolfs.

Together with a letter from Leonard to a subscriber stating that Katherine Mansfield's *Prelude* "is not yet completely printed," though it will be ready shortly, and noting that "four or five copies" of "The Mark on the Wall" are still available.

49. Virginia Woolf, *Wood Is a Pleasant Thing to Think About...*

From *The Mark on the Wall*

London: The Chelsea Book Club, ca. 1921
Private collection

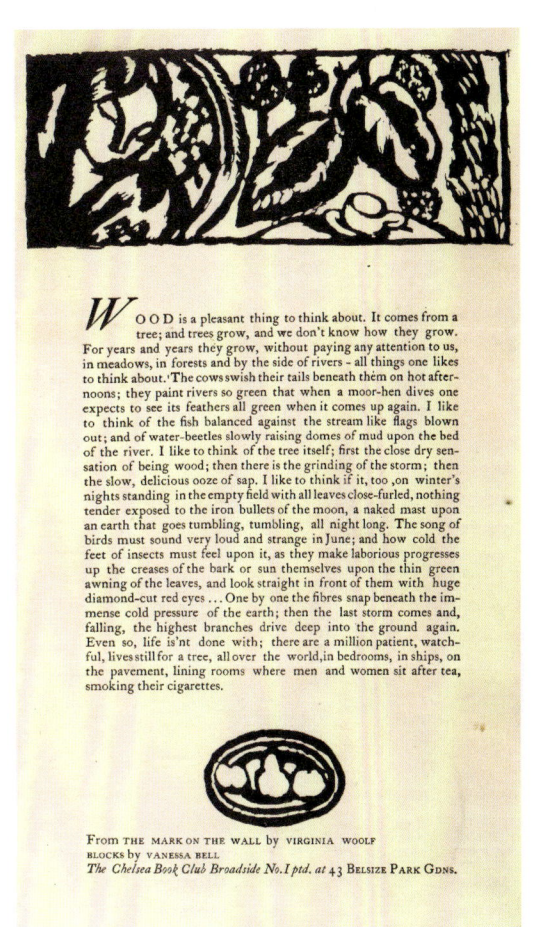

Extract from the final paragraph of her revised version of her story "The Mark on the Wall." Though in its 1917 appearance in *Two Stories* "The Mark on the Wall" was illustrated by Carrington woodcuts, this version is decorated with two woodcuts by Vanessa. It is unclear what circumstances conspired to see this publication fabricated by the Chelsea Book Club, rather than the Hogarth Press, but it exemplifies a style sympathetic to the textual and visual mix of Hogarth publications and may have been printed by John Rodker.
(Kirkpatrick 2c)

50. The Hogarth Press, *Handwritten invoice to Lytton Strachey*

November 11, 1924

Mortimer Rare Book Room, Smith College

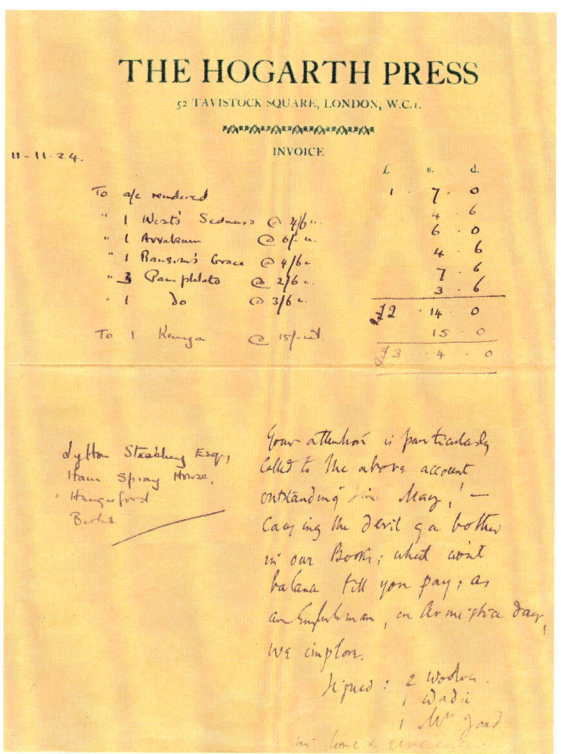

A statement of account addressed to Lytton at Ham Spray House on November 11, 1924, with the following note in Virginia's hand:

Your attention is particularly called to the above account outstanding since May! – carrying the devil of a bother in our Books; which won't balance till you pay; as an Englishman, on Armistice Day, we implore.

> Signed: 2 Woolfs
> 1 Dadie
> 1 Mrs. Joad
> In love and reverence

According to the statement Strachey had purchased Vita's *Seducers in Ecuador*, *The Life of the Archpriest Avvakum*, Ransom's *Grace after Meat*, three pamphlets, and the second edition of Norman Leys's *Kenya*, bringing his total to 3 40p. Marjorie Joad, included on the invoice with Leonard and Virginia and Dadie, worked at the Press from 1923 to 1925.

51. The Hogarth Press, *Complete Catalogue of Books*

Published by the Hogarth Press from 1917 to 1927
London: The Hogarth Press, 1927
Private collection

The Hogarth Press, *Complete Catalogue of Publications*

Arranged under subjects to the Summer of 1939
London: The Hogarth Press, 1939
Private collection

Two catalogues printed to promote their backlist, one called the "first edition" in 1927 and the other, a "new edition," issued over a decade later.

The 1927 volume, published in the eleventh year of the Press, boasts a charming two-page foreword in which an anonymous editor – certainly Leonard or Virginia – puts forth a loose history of the early years of the Press: "The Hogarth Press is now, in its eleventh year, a publishing firm producing its yearly tale of volumes in the manner of other publishers. But it began as a small hand-printing machine worked as a hobby by two amateur and incompetent printers ..." (3). Virginia writes of the step "which, almost unintentionally, turned the Press into a regular publishing business" in 1920, and declares that "[t]he catalogue of our publications which follows will show the way in which this development has taken place. It may be pointed out, however, that the feature with which the Press started still exists and will continue to exist. We still, every year, publish a sprinkling of thin volumes which we print ourselves in our spare time," this catalogue being a case in point: is the upside-down *f* in "feature" a joke, or a symptom? "We print them because we believe – and the past ten years have confirmed our belief – that some of the best and most original work of our time is, in the beginning at least, almost unmarketable..." (4).

The foreword to the 1939 volume, largely cribbed, likely by Lehmann, from the earlier work, updates it in a final paragraph: "In the spring of 1938, Virginia Woolf retired from partnership, and her interests were taken over by John Lehmann. The sole partners in the Hogarth Press now, therefore, are Leonard Woolf and John Lehmann, but on literary questions they have the benefit of the advice of the following distinguished authors: W. H. Auden, Christopher Isherwood, Rosamond Lehmann, V. Sackville-West, Stephen Spender, and Virginia Woolf" (6). The final two pages of the volume (pp. 37-38), listing the International Psycho Analytical Library, is heavily annotated, with markings suggesting that a large number of the Freud publications had gone out of print since the publication of the catalogue. Lehmann joined the Press as a manager in 1931, staying less than a year. He returned in 1938, as stated above, when he bought Virginia's interest in the Press for £3,000 and thus became a full partner with Leonard.

52. T. S. Eliot, *The Waste Land*
Richmond: The Hogarth Press, 1923
Private collection

First English edition, much of it set by Virginia herself, and printed in a run of about 460 copies; preceded by Boni & Liveright's 1922 edition (Woolmer 28, Gallup A6c). The text was demanding, with passages in Greek, Latin, French, and German, and with pages of footnotes larded with italicized citations. Eliot entered Bloomsbury in 1915 when Bertrand Russell introduced him to Ottoline Morrell. He began to associate with several of her literary friends and members of the Bloomsbury set – much to the chagrin of his friends and cohorts Pound and Wyndham Lewis. Late in 1918 Eliot met the Woolfs. Virginia found him "a polished, cultivated, elaborate young American... beneath the surface, it is fairly evident that he is very intellectual, intolerant, with strong views of his own, & a poetic creed." In her diary she commented on the structure and language of a few poems he had shown them.[62] As their friendship evolved they shared a complex mixture of artistic awe and critical intimidation, though in 1921 she wrote, "I am disappointed to find that I am not longer afraid of him,"[63] and by 1922 they were calling him "Tom." (That said, at some point they agreed to cease commenting on each other's work. When, in 1940, she received from him a copy of *East Coker*, she replied, "According to our compact, I say nothing of the printed matter."[64])

In June 1922 "Tom" came to dinner and, Virginia reports in her diary, "read his poem":

> He sang it & chanted it rhythmed it. It has great beauty & force of phrase: symmetry; & tensity. What connects it together, I'm not so sure. But he read till he had to rush. One was left, however,

with some strong emotion. The Waste Land, it is called; & Mary Hutch[inson], who has heard it more quietly, interprets it to be Tom's autobiography – a melancholy one.[65]

Having agreed to publish it months earlier, they were much encouraged by this reading. Having finally set the complicated type, however, in May 1923, Virginia initially expressed primarily relief. The Woolfs often felt frustration at Eliot's reserve and conservatism and, in his autobiography, Leonard admits his bafflement at Eliot's religiosity. None of this, however, prevented Eliot from submitting works for publication and reading them his works in progress, or from suggesting that they publish Joyce's *Ulysses* (they did not: Virginia called it "an illiterate, underbred book"[66]). For their part, the Woolfs nurtured and supported Eliot. Later in 1922, Virginia was involved in an abortive scheme with Ottoline to establish a fund for him, so that he could leave his bank job in favor of writing full-time. Leonard had a more relaxed and professional rapport with him throughout their relationship, especially under the aegis of the *Athenaeum*, and later the *Nation*, which Leonard edited and in which he published Eliot frequently. He stood as one of Eliot's sponsors for British citizenship in 1927.

53. Virginia Woolf, *Monday or Tuesday*

With woodcuts by Vanessa Bell
Richmond: The Hogarth Press, 1921
Private collection

First edition of the only collection of stories Woolf assembled herself. (Leonard published *A Haunted House and Other Short Stories* in 1943.) One thousand copies, the entire edition (Kirkpatrick A5a, Woolmer 17). It prints the following, which Desmond MacCarthy referred to in his *New Statesman* review as "sketches, rhapsodies and meditations": "A Haunted House," "A Society," "Monday or Tuesday," "An Unwritten Novel," "The String Quartet," "Blue and Green," "Kew Gardens," and "The Mark on the Wall" (revised).

As with John Middleton Murry's *The Critic in Judgment* (1919) – the other work they published before they went commercial and started employing outside firms to print longer books – they farmed out this job to F. T. McDermott. Leonard later recollected this as "one of the worst printed books ever published, certainly the worst ever published by the Hogarth Press." The paper McDermott selected he describes as "a nasty spongy antique wove," the amount of ink as "four or five times more" than was necessary or useful. He retells the printing process:

> I have never seen a more desperate, ludicrous – but for me at the time tragic – scene he got so much ink on the blocks and his paper was so soft and spongy that little fluffy bits of paper were torn off with the ink and stuck to the blocks and then to the rollers and finally to the type. We had to stop every few minutes and clean everything, but even so the pages were an appalling sight. We machined 1,000 copies, and at the end we sank down exhausted and speechless on the floor by the side of the machine, where we sat and silently drank beer until I was sufficiently revived to crawl battered and broken back to Hogarth House.

Singing a refrain oft heard, even now, when Vanessa's dust-jackets for her sister's books are discussed, MacCarthy noted in his review that Virginia's text was "accompanied, rather than illustrated, by woodcuts of a rough, blottesque, pleasantly vigorous kind by Vanessa Bell."

Though Woolf later hoped to disown the title story, as well as "Blue and Green," three of her most important literary experiments are included: "An Unwritten Novel," "Kew Gardens," and "The Mark on the Wall." Clive later quite accurately stated, "This is Virginia Woolf practising,"[67] a theory she confirmed in a letter to Smyth:

> These little pieces in *Monday or (and) Tuesday* were written by way of diversion; they were the treats I allowed myself when I had done my exercise in the conventional style. I shall never forget the day I wrote "The Mark on the Wall" – all in a flash, as if flying, after being kept stone breaking for months. "The Unwritten Novel" was the great discovery, however. That – again in one second – showed me how I could embody all my deposit of experience in a shape that fitted it – not that I have ever reached that end; but anyhow I saw, branching out of the tunnel I made, when I discovered that method of approach, *Jacob's Room, Mrs. Dalloway* etc. – How I trembled with excitement; and then Leonard came in, and I drank my milk, and concealed my excitement, and wrote I suppose another page of that interminable *Night and Day* (which some say is my best book).

54. Virginia Woolf, *Jacob's Room*

Richmond: The Hogarth Press, 1922
Private collection

First edition of Woolf's first novel to appear under the Hogarth Press imprint. Twelve hundred copies printed (Kirkpatrick A6a, Woolmer 26). Copies sent to early subscribers of the Press in October 1922 – probably about 40 – had a subscriber's slip signed by Virginia tipped in, as does this copy, which was sent to Lytton Strachey's brother Oliver. The slip reads as follows, with the portions Woolf filled out in black ink added in quotation marks below:

> This copy of "Jacob's Room"
> is issued to "Oliver Strachey Esq"
> as an A Subscriber to The Hogarth Press and
> is therefore signed by the Author: "Virginia Woolf / Oct. 1922."

According to Leonard's initial subscription scheme, "A" subscribers would be sent all Hogarth Press publications automatically, whereas "B" subscribers would be sent a notice of each publication, encouraging them to purchase individual titles.

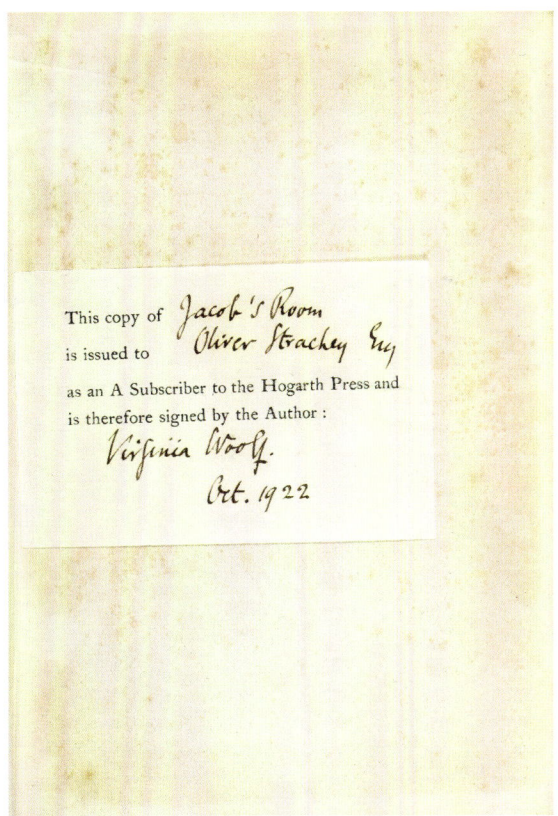

55. Virginia Woolf, *Kew Gardens*
Richmond: The Hogarth Press, 1919
Private collection

Virginia Woolf, *Kew Gardens*
Second edition
Richmond: The Hogarth Press, 1919
Private collection

Virginia Woolf, *Kew Gardens*
Decorated by Vanessa Bell
Third edition
London: The Hogarth Press, 1927
Private collection

The first three editions of Virginia's essay that would result in the most successful collaboration between her and Vanessa. The Woolfs printed just 150 copies of the first edition, and after seven earlier titles clearly believed their audience would be primarily friends and colleagues: the colophon that reads "L. and V. Woolf" is pasted over a less formal one on the final page that reads, simply, "Leonard and Virginia." The covers were made from paper hand-colored in orange, brown, and blue at the Omega Workshops, and bear a pasted-on label. Despite its haphazard production values – Rhein notes that "its printing is unbelievably poor and the states are a bibliographic nightmare,"[68] and bibliographers are still untangling the variations in size and state of the woodcuts – it was received so positively by the *TLS* that an immediate reprinting by a commercial printer was needed: "here is a thing of original and therefore strange beauty, with its own atmosphere, its own vital force . . . the more one gloats over 'Kew Gardens' the more beauty shines out of it." Leonard recalls in *Beginning Again*,

> When we opened the front door of Hogarth House [after returning from a week in the country during which the *Times* review appeared], we found the hall covered with envelopes and postcards containing orders from booksellers all over the country. It was impossible for us to start printing enough copies to meet these orders. . . .

Five hundred wrapped copies were prepared immediately, and the verso of the title page reads, "First Published, May, 1919. Second Edition, June 1919."

Those first two editions included a frontispiece and tailpiece by Vanessa, and their production caused serious family quarrels. At one point, Virginia wrote in her diary, Vanessa "firmly refused to illustrate any more stories of mine under those circumstances & went so far as to doubt the value of the Hogarth Press altogether ." In 1927, however, the Woolfs issued a new edition, in a limited, large-paper format and with a cover design and new decorations, unique to each page, by Vanessa. That edition bears out Virginia's initial view, discussed with Roger Fry, that the written and visual arts could indeed be different expressions of a similar spirit.

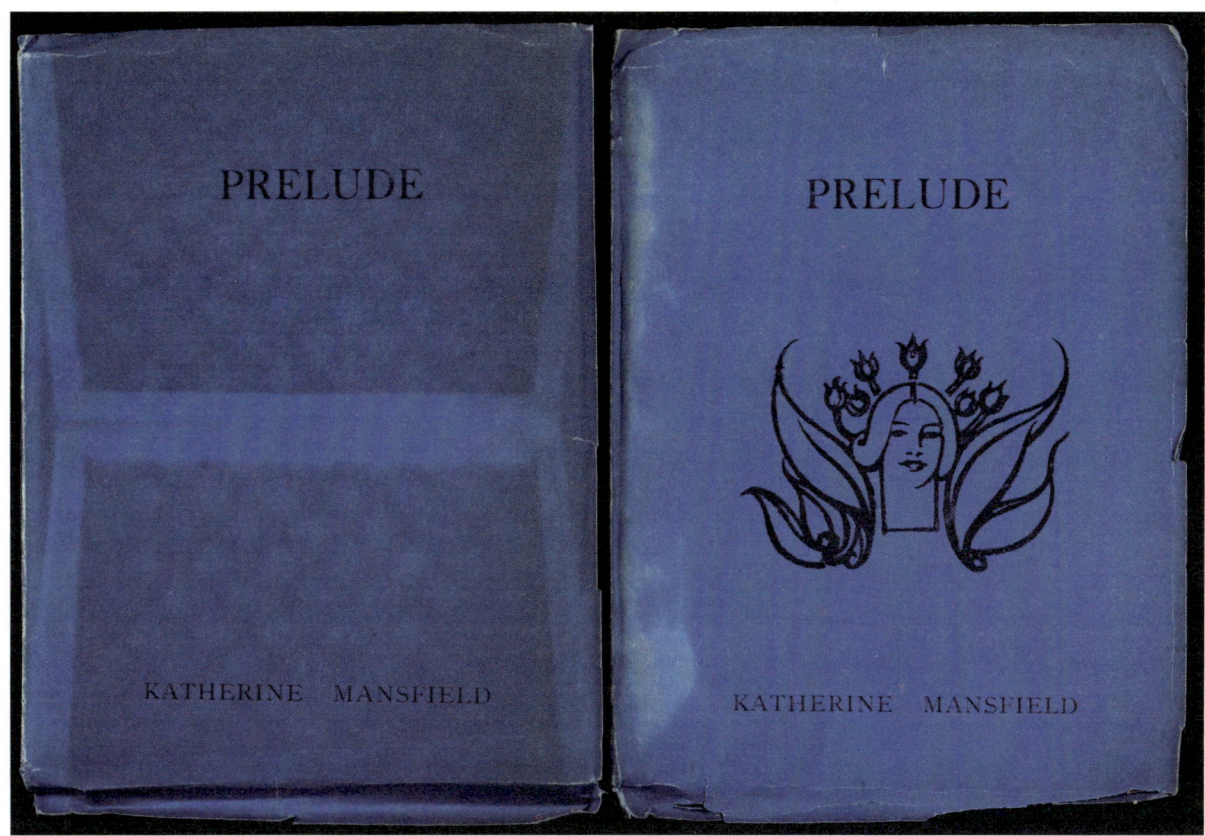

56. Katherine Mansfield, *Prelude*

Richmond: The Hogarth Press, 1918
Private collection

Two first editions of Mansfield's story: one bearing J. D. Fergusson's line block, selected by Mansfield but disliked and therefore dropped by Woolf, on the front wrapper, and one without. Three hundred copies were printed altogether, but few with the cover illustration. Virginia may have set the type herself; records are unclear (Woolmer 2).

Hand-printed and published by the Woolfs (though on the larger press of a fellow printer) and intended to be the second book brought out by the Press, *Prelude* was delayed for the publication of C. N. S. Woolf's *Poems*, brought to the Press by Leonard's brother Philip on March 7, 1918, and quickly done up as a memorial.

57. Virginia Woolf, *Autograph letter signed to Katherine Mansfield*

February 13, 1921
Mortimer Rare Book Room, Smith College

Virginia struck up an intimacy with Katherine several months after the publication of *Prelude*, and had a tentative relationship with her throughout her career. In this letter, she responds to a communication from Katherine, discussing friends, Katherine's recently published *Bliss*, the promise of women writers, and her own jealousy:

> I was so delighted to get your letter. It came as I was having my tea alone – a half spring evening, rather pale, & a bunch of mimosa something very sweet. I read it twice & then I read the envelope – I saw Murry two nights ago when I dined at Gordon Square; but Clive bawls so that one can scarcely say anything – still, we talked a little about you, which I liked. I'm always thinking of things to say to you. They have to be put in my diary. I'm wondering what you think about your book what people have said about it. The reviews are enthusiastic, but then the reviews are stupid. Shall I write you a criticism yet one of these days? I sometimes think that though we're so different we have some of the same difficulties. I'm in the middle of my novel now, but have to break off, of course, to make a little money . What I admire in you so much is your transparent quality. My stuff gets muddy & then in a novel we must have continuity, but in this one I'm always chipping & changing from one level to another, I think what I'm at is to change the consciousness & so to break up the awful stodge . And you seem to me to go so straightly & directly – all clear as glass – refined. But I must read them over again properly. I feel as if I didn't want just all realism any more – only thoughts & feelings – no cups & tables .
>
> Like an idiot I lost my temper with Arnold Bennett for abusing women & wasted my time writing a foolish violent, I suppose unnecessary satire. Somehow it seems to me worse than lazy impertinence on his part. Suppose some poor wretch who wanted to write was put off by that little grocer? And so I lashed out. It seems to me very important that women should learn to write. Does it to you?
>
> God knows I don't much like them when they do it – or men either for the matter of that . I said Damn Katherine! Why can't I be the only woman who knows how to write?

She writes of her efforts to keep out of the literary scene, and then in the next sentence sends news of all her literary friends – Tom Eliot, Lytton Strachey – not to mention "our memoir club, which gets more and more brilliant and more and more unreal . But I must say of my friends that with all their faults they get nicer with success ."

Mansfield died in early January 1923 of a pulmonary hemorrhage. She was 34 years old. Virginia wrote to Mansfield's intimate, Dorothy Brett, days after, "I wanted to write you about Katherine, but all I could say seemed futile; but that does not mean that my feeling is. I am glad to find how many of her letters I have . . ."[69] She begins the project of typing out Katherine's letters, and laments her own missed opportunities, "wasted chances," to become a closer friend.[70] To Ottoline Morrell in 1928 she wrote, "I'm reading Katherine Mansfield's letters and feel desolated by them. What a waste! – and how wretched it is – her poverty, her illness – I didn't realize how gifted she was either. And now never to – but you well know all I mean."[71]

58. Robert Louis Stevenson, *Familiar Studies of Men and Books*
London: Chatto & Windus, 1912
Private collection

"Fine-paper edition" of this collection of essays that began life in *Cornhill* and other magazines and saw their first book publication in 1882. In his preface Stevenson writes that these studies – of Victor Hugo, Robert Burns, Walt Whitman, Henry David Thoreau, Yoshida-Torajiro, François Villon, Charles of Orleans, Samuel Pepys, and "John Knox and Women" – are the writings of "a literary vagrant": "One book led to another, one study to another." They appeared in a variety of monthly periodicals. However, he is especially grateful to *Cornhill*, to which he owes "a double debt of thanks; first, that I was received there in the very best society, and under the eye of the very best of editors" – presumably, Leslie Stephen – "and second, that the proprietors have allowed me to republish so considerable an amount of copy."

Virginia covered this volume with a cream-patterned paper with an abstract floral motif – a paper selected, no doubt, for its echo of the green and white floral endpapers – and affixed a handwritten label to the spine: *R.L. Stevenson / Familiar Studies of Men & Books*.

Nathaniel Hawthorne, *The House of the Seven Gables*
London . . . : Humphrey Milford/Oxford University Press, 1924
Private collection

Published as part of the World's Classics series; the first edition was published in 1851. Julian Bell's copy, with his ownership signature on the front pastedown, *JBell*, offset onto the front endpaper, and Virginia's hand-lettered spine. An interesting choice of gift: Hawthorne spelled out the "moral" of the book in the preface: "that the wrong-doing of one generation lives into the successive ones, and, divesting itself of every temporary advantage, becomes a pure and uncontrollable mischief. . . ." It is difficult, reading this, not to think of Julian's lament, writing to Aunt Virginia from China, that his upbringing in Bloomsbury did not prepare him for any proper "job" in life. Woolf's appreciation for Hawthorne began with her early exposure to him through her father. She recalled "scribbling a story in the manner of Hawthorne" as a young girl[72] and later plunged into Hawthorne's works.

The present volume's original cloth binding is covered in what appears to be hand block-printed paper – of the type used in the early editions that came from the Hogarth Press. Virginia carefully lettered the paper label on the spine: *House of Seven Gables / Hawthorne.*

Virginia began seriously pursuing bookbinding as a therapeutic pastime in 1901, when she initiated a series of more or less casual lessons. Though she seems to have requested instruction sporadically during the next few years, just six months after her first visit to the bindery of Sylvia Stebbing she wrote to Thoby, "I am really rather a good binder," and requested some volumes on which to experiment. Alan Isaac explores the roots of what she called her "career" as a binder, attributing a great deal of her aesthetic vision to Fry's influence:

> For Fry the joy of creation should infuse the work. It should be vital and spontaneous. "Meaning for him came not through the perfecting of a technique but in the opportunity to create."

Much the same principles can be applied to Virginia's bookbinding. It is too simplistic to say that Virginia's "own efforts at book repair are slapdash and pathetically inadequate." She probably did work at speed, but is it reasonable to conclude that she was clumsy and incapable? She did not, on her own admission, dedicate herself to the craft of book binding and devote the time to the practice which would have been necessary to increase her skill. She was, therefore, generally technically poor; paper and boards sometimes appearing to have been chosen at random. Her binding, she knew, was "amateurish."

Isaac attributes the attention-grabbing covers of *Kew Gardens* and other Hogarth Press productions to Virginia's earliest experiments in bookbinding. In 1902 she wrote, "There seem ever so many ways of making covers – of leather-linen-silk-parchment-vellum-japanese paper etc. etc. etc. which the ordinary lidders never think of."[73] Leonard later recalled, "for many years we gave much time and care to finding beautiful, uncommon and sometimes cheerful paper for binding our books . We got papers from all over the place, including some brilliantly patterned from Czechoslovakia, and we also had some marbled covers made for us by Roger Fry's daughter in Paris."

VIa. Her Literature

Mrs. Dalloway

Mrs. Dalloway
London: The Hogarth Press, 1925
In the jacket designed by Vanessa Bell
Private collection

"The Central Things"

Sarah Funke

Mrs. Dalloway, with *To the Lighthouse*, tops the list of Woolf's most popular and readable examples of her sustained literary experiments. The narrative follows Clarissa Dalloway around London on a day mid-June 1923 as she arranges party details, and the reader is privy to her thoughts and memories. As Clarissa thinks of or passes by Woolf's other characters, the narration jumps from her head to theirs. The strong counterpoint to Clarissa's rhythm is provided by Septimus Smith, a shell-shock victim pushed to the verge of suicide despite (or, the implication is, perhaps because of) the myopic ministrations of the self-absorbed psychiatrist – and Dalloway party guest – Sir William Bradshaw, an amalgam of the several incompetent psychiatrists Woolf herself had encountered when trying to allay her mental unrest. Woolf developed Septimus's wife Rezia from impressions she had of the Russian-born ballet dancer Lydia Lopokova (John Maynard Keynes's wife), and took elements of Clarissa's daughter Elizabeth from her own youth. Other important characters emerge from Clarissa's past: Peter Walsh, whose marriage proposal she turned down long ago but who has unexpectedly returned to see her; and Sally Seton, the most intimate companion of her adolescence, inspired by her own first love: Margaret Symonds Vaughan.

Clarissa Dalloway made her brief but colorful debut in *The Voyage Out* (1915); appeared more fully in "Mrs. Dalloway in Bond Street" in *Dial* (1923); and was, according to some critics, a changed woman in her incarnation in the short but powerful novel that appeared in 1925.

After working in fits and starts for months, Woolf declared her work in progress "a study of insanity & suicide: the world seen by the sane & the insane side by side – something like that." Nine months later, she confided a critical self-examination to her journal: "In this book I have almost too many ideas."

> I want to give life & death, sanity & insanity; I want to criticise the social system, & to show it at work, at its most intense – But here I may be posing. Am I writing The Hours [its working title] from deep emotion? Of course the mad part tries me so much, makes my mind squint so badly that I can hardly face spending the next weeks at it. Have I the power of conveying the true reality? Or do I write essays about myself? I think it most important in this book to go for the central things, even though they don't submit, as they should however, to beautification in language.

Woolf toiled for two years on *Mrs. Dalloway*, off and on, taking time for the compilation of *The Common Reader*. Despite occasional moments of doubt and distress, she was aware that she had struck stylistic gold. "The design is so queer & so masterful. The design is certainly original, & interests me hugely."[74] She described the "discovery" of her method: "I dig out beautiful caves behind my characters; I think that gives exactly what I want; humanity, humour, depth.

The idea is that the caves shall connect, & each comes to daylight at the present moment – Dinner!" She called it one of her "most tantalising & refractory of books," noting that "Parts are so bad, parts so good; I'm much interested; can't stop making it up yet – yet."

> I think the design is more remarkable than in any of my books. I daresay I shan't be able to carry it out. I am stuffed with ideas for it. I feel I can use up everything I've ever thought. The doubtful point is I think the character of Mrs. Dalloway. It may be too stiff, too glittering & tinsely – But then I can bring innumerable other characters to her support. I wrote the 100th page today. It took me a year's groping to discover what I call my tunneling process, by which I tell the past by installments, as I have need of it. This is my prime discovery so far... I own I have my hope for this book.[75]

Woolf's friends were to varying degrees impressed and enraptured. Lytton was the most critical of the group:

> No, Lytton does not like Mrs. Dalloway, and, what is odd, I like him all the better for saying so, and don't much mind. What he says is that there is a discordancy between the ornament (extremely beautiful) and what happens (rather ordinary – or unimportant). This is caused, he thinks, by some discrepancy in Clarissa herself: he thinks she is disagreeable and limited, but that I alternately laugh at her and cover her, very remarkably, with myself. What can one call it but genius? he said! Fuller of genius, he said, than anything I had done. Perhaps, he said, you have not yet mastered your method.

Arnold Bennett, with whom she had been exchanging thrusts for years, predictably wrote that this "beat" him: "I could not finish it, because I could not discover what it was really about, what was its direction, and what Mrs. Woolf intended to demonstrate by it. I failed to discern what was its moral basis. As regards character-drawing, Mrs. Woolf (in my opinion) told us ten thousand things about Mrs. Dalloway, but did not show us Mrs. Dalloway. Nor could I see much trace of construction, or ordered movement towards a climax, either in *Jacob's Room* or *Mrs. Dalloway*. Further, I thought that both books seriously lacked vitality." He added that these defects constituted "the characteristic defects of the new school of which Mrs. Woolf is the leader. The people in them do not sufficiently live, and hence they cannot claim our sympathy or even our hatred: they leave us indifferent." He concluded, "In the novels of Mrs. Woolf some brief passages are so exquisitely done that nothing could be done better. But to be fine for a few minutes is not enough. The chief proof of first-rateness is sustained power."

E. M. Forster was more positive, declaring it "perhaps her masterpiece, but difficult... visual sensitiveness – in itself a slight tool for a novelist – becomes in her case a productive force." One of the shrewdest assessments comes from contemporary biographer Hermione Lee:

> *Mrs. Dalloway* (1925), her most dramatic mixing of autobiography and history, puts to shame the idea of starting afresh in a New World "now that it was all over, truce signed, and the dead buried." We see a society divided between those who have profited from the war and those who, like Septimus Smith, have been destroyed by it. The war lives in dreams, madness, memory. A

grey nurse knitting on a park bench becomes, in the dream of one of the characters, a gigantic symbolic shape looming over the book, "the figure of the mother whose sons have been killed in the battles of the world."

Without question with *Mrs. Dalloway* Woolf turned the corner to permanent public recognition. By June 1925 it had outsold in its first year *Jacob's Room*, and her friends were "enthusiastic – really so, I think; & ready to acclaim me successful, arrived, triumphant with this book: Clive, Mary, Molly, Roger, my latest allies." A month later reviews were still coming in, positive and negative, and sales had picked up; on July 19, 1925, she noted, "the *Calendar* has abused Mrs. D. which hurt me a little; & then the tide of praise has flowed over me again, & they both sell well, & my fears were ungrounded."

59. Charlotte M. Yonge, *The Little Duke. Richard the Fearless*
With illustrations
London and New York: Macmillan and Co., 1895
Private collection

First edition, with 40 pages of undated publisher's ads in the rear. A gift copy, inscribed in a confident, flowing hand on the first blank to a fourteen-year-old Virginia by her first love, Margaret Symonds Vaughan, the model for Sally Seton: *For Ginia. From a terrified and terrifying Chief. May 19th, 96.* "Madge" Vaughan, a daughter of John Aldington Symonds, was Virginia's childhood intimate and confidante, and eventually became related by marriage – she wed William Wymar Vaughan, one of Virginia's orphaned Vaughan cousins with whom she was close in her youth; Emma Vaughan became, in fact, one of Virginia's most active adult correspondents. The nickname "Chief" derives from a winter visit to Hyde Park Gate when Virginia was a child; the moniker, used in this inscription seven years later, clearly stuck. Quentin describes the compelling, somewhat enigmatic figure the 20-year-old Madge cast:

> She had grown up among the Swiss mountains in an atmosphere of freedom, she was a writer, she was passionately interested in the arts – and there was something melancholy about her. Her father's death in 1893 had hit her very hard and she had an intense capacity for suffering. But there was also something childlike, wondering and fresh about her attitude to life. She was modern, adventurous, 'aesthetic' – very much a girl of the 'nineties, and this inevitably was attractive; and then she was herself attractive.

The feelings the young Virginia – thirteen years her junior – developed were intense:

> Virginia was in fact in love with her. Certainly it was a very pure and very intense passion – pure in almost every sense of the word; Virginia at sixteen was by modern standards almost unbelievably ignorant. It was pure also in its sincerity, in its lack of jealous feeling. It was the passion of a girl in a junior form for a dashing senior, not a passion based upon intimacy.[76]

The relationship did not survive much beyond Virginia's adolescence, during which the two wrote frequently, sometimes offering literary ideas and even manuscript material for critique. Virginia once referred to Madge's missives, along with those of Vanessa, as "the most interesting letters" in her possession. However, Madge's career lacked the focus and intensity – and, ultimately, the success – of Virginia's, and the two grew apart. Madge never achieved more than a fraction of the creative and intellectual potential Virginia had first admired in her, and her disappointment and disillusionment must have been acute. Virginia wrote in 1917 to a friend: "I wish you *could* make Madge write. Perhaps she'd be happier then, though I don't think anything could make Madge really happy; it's not in the Symonds nature ."[77] Madge did continue to write, if not as fruitfully as did Virginia, who tactfully declined the opportunity to review her 1920 work, *A Child of the Alps*. Madge died in 1925, by which time the two, it appears, had stopped corresponding entirely.

60. Ottoline Morrell, *Virginia Woolf*

Garsington, 1923

Mortimer Rare Book Room, Smith College

Lady Ottoline Morrell, a generous and intellectually ambitious hostess, played a pivotal role in bringing together the artistic and intellectual lights of the period, first through Thursday evening cultural gatherings – taking over, in a way, those evenings initiated by Thoby and Vanessa – and later by providing safe-haven on her farm at Garsington to conscientious objectors (such as Bertrand Russell) during the First World War. She was less productive, perhaps, than her Bloomsbury friends, but no less sexually adventurous. While married to Philip Morrell she had an affair with Bertrand Russell, a flirtation with Roger Fry, and creative relationships with a number of others.

Virginia, whose diaries and even, arguably, some passages of *Mrs. Dalloway* evince – like communications between her and Lytton and others of their circle – both admiration and scorn for the oddly beautiful and eccentric lady, was drawn into a fairly close and warm friendship that lasted for years, until Ottoline's death in 1938. Virginia wrote in her obituary for the *Times* that "'the great lady who suddenly appeared in the world of artists and writers before the War easily lent herself to caricature,' and that the ridicule of her friends overlooked the complexity of her nature."[78]

61. Virginia Woolf, *Mrs. Dalloway*

Manuscript outline, October 6, 1922

The Henry W. and Albert A. Berg Collection of English and American Literature, Astor Lenox and Tilden Foundations, The New York Public Library

A one-page manuscript outline for *Mrs. Dalloway*, composed by Virginia in the third notebook of her *Jacob's Room* manuscript. She begins, "thoughts upon beginning a book to be called, perhaps, At Home: or The Party: This is to be a short book consisting of six or seven chapters each completely separately [*sic*] but there must be some sort of fusion, and all must converge upon the party at the end." The characters of *Mrs. Dalloway*, and others, will be "much in relief," with "interludes of thought, or reflection, or short digressions (which must be related, logically, to the rest) all compact, yet not jerked." She lists eight chapters, and remarks that each could be roughed out in a month's time. She concludes, "There should be some fun."

62. Virginia Woolf, *Mrs. Dalloway in Bond Street*
Typescript excerpt
The Henry W. and Albert A. Berg Collection of English and American
Literature, Astor Lenox and Tilden Foundations, The New York Public Library

Virginia Woolf, *Mrs. Dalloway in Bond Street*
In *The Dial* LXXV.1 (July 1923), pp. 20-27
Private collection

First leaf of a 23-page corrected typescript, showing the work in one of its many stages; typed yet full of Virginia's manuscript emendations, as she crosses out, changes, and inserts words and phrases, in purple ink and in black, suggesting at least two rounds of review. In the first sentence she initially wrote that Clarissa would "buy the silk" herself; she changed this by hand to "gloves," and in the first edition Clarissa decides to buy the flowers herself. Together with a copy of its published state.

63. *Virginia Woolf, Dadie Rylands*
September 1934
Reprinted by permission of the Harvard Theatre Collection, The Houghton Library

George Humphrey Wolferstan "Dadie" Rylands, whose nickname dates to his childhood, was one in a parade of assistants Leonard and Virginia apprenticed at the Hogarth Press. One of the youngest members of the Bloomsbury Group, he grew to be a revered figure at Cambridge University. Over the years he became a Fellow, teacher, and Shakespeare scholar, and according to his obituary in the *Times*, "[G]enerations of undergraduates knew him as a wise confidant with a great understanding of human follies and frailties."

Through his friendship with Lytton, Rylands joined the Press in July 1924. Virginia wrote to Ottoline, "Dadie has arrived, very charming, but with no knowledge, naturally, of how to write a bill." He also struck her as "a corncoloured youth" and "a very nice boy," and, years later, as "pink as a daisy and as proud as a wood-lion." In November 1924 she sketched his entrée into Bloomsbury:

> About the young man in the basement, George Rylands. Alas, he will soon cease to be in the basement, King's College requiring him to work harder at his dissertation, and so he will be going after Xmas to write upon Diction in Poetry, and so win a fellowship, and live at Cambridge and teach, which they now insist on – rather a nuisance for us. He is a semi-Neo Pagan perhaps. At King's they are all reminded of Rupert [Brooke] – partly his yellow hair, partly his poetry, which is not so good as Rupert's. He is a very charming spoilt boy, sprung of the rich who have no money, and so rather dazzled by London and parties and perhaps he scents himself; but at heart he is uncorrupted, (so I think – others disagree) and all young and oldish men, fall in love with him, and he dines out every night, and treats his lovers abominably. However, if he don't [sic] get his fellowship, he will come back here, if possible.

Though Rylands's tenure at the Press was one of the shortest among the assistants, the friendship he formed with the Woolfs was lasting. While they printed the books of their well-known literary and intellectual companions, they also gave a boost to young talent, especially when it appeared in as appealing a package as Dadie. After he returned to Cambridge University, where in 1922 he had been elected an Apostle, the Woolfs would publish three of his books: *Russet and Taffeta* (1925), which he dedicated to Virginia; his Cambridge dissertation, *Words and Poetry* (1928); and *Poems* (1931).

The parties Dadie hosted in his Cambridge rooms, decorated by Carrington and Douglas Davidson, are legendary. Virginia immortalized one of his luncheons in *A Room of One's Own*.

64. Virginia Woolf, *Mrs. Dalloway*

London: The Hogarth Press, 1925
Private collection

First edition. A presentation copy, inscribed on the front endpaper: *Dadie from Virginia,* with Rylands's bookplate on the front paste-down.

VIb. Her Literature
To the Lighthouse

To the Lighthouse
London: The Hogarth Press, 1927
In the jacket designed by Vanessa Bell
Private collection

"Flown with Words"

by Sarah Funke

Virginia felt that with *To the Lighthouse* she might have perfected her craft. It is divided into three parts, all set at the Ramsay summer home in the Hebrides, and incorporating elements of Virginia's childhood summer retreats. The first part, "The Window," consumes almost a full day before the war. The final part, "The Lighthouse," pictures a morning after the war, at the end of a decade-long vacancy. These two sections are divided by "Time Passes," which covers the ten years during which the house was empty. It is for this section that she received the most attention and the greatest accolades, first for the 1926 appearance in French in a Paris periodical in a translation by Charles Mauron, and then upon publication of the novel.

The Ramsay family was a clear stand-in for the Stephens: with eight children (unlike the Stephens, all from the same mother), the head of the household was immediately recognizable as Leslie Stephen, and Mrs. Ramsay, as an imaginative vision of Julia:

> This is going to be fairly short: to have father's character done completely in it; & mothers; & St. Ives; & childhood; & all the usual things I try to put in – life, death &c. But the centre is father's character, sitting in a boat, reciting We perished, each alone, while he crushes a dying mackerel.[79]

Two years later she admitted to Vita Sackville-West: "I don't know if I'm like Mrs. Ramsay: as my mother died when I was 13 probably it is a child's view of her: but I have some sentimental delight in thinking that you like her. She has haunted me: but then so did that old wretch my father: I was more like him than her, I think; and therefore more critical: but he was an adorable man, and somehow, tremendous."

Beginning in May 1925 with this idea for the subject matter, and the assertion that the form it would take would be completely new, she confessed in July that she might have to "invent a new name for the book to supplant 'novel'. A new — by Virginia Woolf. But what? Elegy?" Seven months later she wrote of her success: "at last, after that battle *Jacob's Room*, that agony – all agony but the end, *Mrs. Dalloway*, I am now writing as fast & freely as I have written in the whole of my life; more so – 20 times more so – than any novel yet. I think this is the proof that I was on the right path; & that what fruit hangs in my soul is to be reached there. I live entirely in it, & come to the surface rather obscurely." That September she added, "I think it is subtler & more human than *J[acob's] R[oom]* & *Mrs. D[alloway]*..." concluding, "It is proved, I think, that what I have to say is to be said in this manner." A month later she was of the same mind: "My present opinion is that it is easily the best of my books, fuller than *J.'s R.* and less spasmodic, occupied with more interesting things than *Mrs D.* and not complicated with all that desperate accompaniment of madness. It is freer and subtler I think."

She suspected fairly early on that "Time Passes" would dwarf her other achievements; she called it "this impersonal thing, which I'm dared to do by my friends, the flight of time, and the consequent break of unity in my design. That passage interests me very much. A new problem like that breaks fresh ground in one's mind; prevents the regular ruts." After months of thought and experimentation, she defined the section in her diary:

> [H]ere is the most difficult abstract piece of writing – I have to give an empty house, no people's characters, the passage of time, all eyeless and featureless with nothing to cling to: well, I rush at it, and at once scatter out two pages. Is it nonsense, is it brilliance? Why am I so flown with words, and apparently free to do exactly what I like? When I read a bit it seems spirited too; needs compressing, but not much else.

She finished the first draft on September 13, 1926, and began revisions in November, noting that she was rewriting six pages a day, and removing substantial autobiographical material. After its completion she wrote in her diary, "I am anxious about Time Passes. Think the whole thing may be pronounced soft, shallow, insipid, sentimental."

After publication, she recalled years later, she fell into an emotional and mental lethargy: "After *Lighthouse* I was I remember nearer suicide, seriously, than since 1913 after the first divine relief, of course some terrible blankness must spread."

Her closest friends and best critics all offered exuberant praise except Roger Fry who, she wrote in her diary, "it is clear did not like Time Passes," despite the revisions she had made in response to his prepublication critique. Leonard thought it was her best book and a "masterpiece": "He calls it entirely new, 'a psychological poem', is his name for it." And though *Harpers* and *The Forum* refused serial rights, and she perceived Harcourt Brace to be "a good deal less enthusiastic" than they had been about *Mrs. Dalloway*, the prepublication sales figure approached 1,700 – double that of the earlier novel. A less than luminous review in the *TLS* – "an exact copy of the *JSR Mrs. Dalloway* review, gentlemanly, kindly, timid & praising beauty, doubting character, and leaving me moderately depressed" – did nothing to hinder sales. By June they had sold 2,200 copies and were reprinting. By July they had exhausted the first printing, and were dipping into the second. Forster wrote, "It is awfully sad, very beautiful; it stirs me much more to questions of whether and why than anything else you have written. I am inclined to think it your best work." Even Fry told her that despite his reservations about "Time Passes" it was the best of her work to date; like Leonard, he felt it was specifically better than *Mrs. Dalloway*. Woolf replied that Fry had "kept me on the right path, so far as writing goes, more than anyone."

65. Stella Duckworth?, *Julia Stephen and the Stephen Children*

Drawing room, Talland House, St. Ives, Cornwall
Ca. 1894

Mortimer Rare Book Room, Smith College

Vanessa, Adrian, and Virginia and Thoby seated in front in the drawing room at St. Ives, at lessons with their mother. Possibly captured on film by Stella.

66. Virginia Woolf, *To the Lighthouse*

Manuscript

The Henry W. and Albert A. Berg Collection of English and American Literature, Astor Lenox and Tilden Foundations, The New York Public Library

One of three volumes of an early manuscript draft, containing a loose leaf of chapter list, a title page, diary entries of progress, a list of character names, and the opening chapters of the text. On August 6, 1925, Virginia writes, "The plan of this book is roughly that it shall consist of three parts." The first establishes the characters of Mr. and Mrs. Ramsay, and their relationship. She then discusses the second part, one of the most controversial writing projects of her career: "2. The passing of time. I am not sure how this is to be given: an interesting experiment, giving the sense of 10 years passing." She concludes, "3. This is the voyage to the lighthouse. Reveal characters can be brought in: the young atheist. The old gentleman; the lovers: episodes can be written on woman's beauty; on truth: " but "making a more harmonious whole" than in *Mrs. Dalloway*. "Whether this will be long or short I do not know. The dominating impression is one of Mr. R's character."

67. Virginia Woolf, *To the Lighthouse*

Corrected page proofs
January 13–February 12, 1927
Mortimer Rare Book Room, Smith College

Virginia's page proofs for the English edition, copiously annotated in preparation for its U.S. release.

VII. Her Essays and the Group's Fame

Virginia Woolf, *Time Magazine*,
XXIX.15 (April 12, 1937)

The Chronicler and the Artist Deirdre Bair

The modern biographer reminded Virginia Woolf of a canary in a coal mine, sent in as an early warning detector to ferret out the "falsity, unreality, and obsolete conventions" lurking in the biographical atmosphere.[80] In a sense, she was describing herself in 1934 as she debated if she could muster "the indomitable courage"[81] it would take to write her third biography, of Roger Fry. She knew well the difficulties, for she had already written *Orlando*, the wildly impressionistic life of her lover, Vita Sackville-West, and *Flush*, ostensibly the biography of Elizabeth Barrett Browning's cocker spaniel but in reality a tongue-in-cheek homage to Vita for giving her one called Pinka.

Virginia practiced several maxims from her essay on "The Art of Biography" when she wrote the first two quasi-biographies: that the genre best provides "the truthful transmission of personality" when it is combined with fiction to give "the creative fact; the fact that suggests and engenders." With Roger Fry's life, she planned to count on friends for the basic "facts" and permit herself to create the rest "without any restrictions save those that the artist chooses to obey."

However, Roger's life posed problems for a woman born in 1882 at the height of Victorian convention, even though times had certainly changed by the 1930s. She worried that it contained too many unsavory facts, even though she believed she could overcome them because in biography (as opposed to science) they were "subject to changes of opinion," and "opinion changes as the times change."

Virginia always admired Roger, not only for his career as a distinguished art historian, critic, and lecturer, but also for his generous friendship. He, in his turn, felt such affinity for her writing that he had often expressed interest in her becoming his biographer. Writing about his work would be pleasurable; the difficulty would surround his personal relationships.

When Roger died, she was deep into *The Years*, the novel that many consider her masterpiece and the one most difficult to write. It went through so many incarnations that it had become what Vanessa's son, Quentin Bell, described as "a nightmare."[82] Under such pressure, Virginia was relieved when Roger's sister and literary executor, Margery, proposed that instead of a biography, there should be a collection of essays. Contributors were chosen to represent the different aspects of Roger's life: besides Virginia those writing about his gift for friendship were Clive Bell and his and Vanessa's son, Julian; the art world was represented by the artist Walter Sickert and the art historian Anthony Blunt; the literary world and peace movement by Gerald Heard; and Roger's friend, Nathaniel Wedd, for their years at Cambridge.

As always, the Bloomsbury circle had much to say for and against a compendium versus a traditional biography. Ottoline Morrell, herself a woman of highly liberated behavior, was against the revelations inherent in any form of biographical writing; Julian Bell, who knew of his mother's passionate affair with Roger, agreed with Ottoline. Everyone was surprised when Vanessa said she preferred a traditional biography and was eager for Virginia to write it.

Virginia was not so sure. She worried about how to write of Roger's sexual proclivities when she had such difficulty writing about mere emotional friendships in her novels. Writing Roger's life would require a fairly full discussion of his unconventional affairs, especially with Vanessa, which Virginia feared would only call attention to her sister's other notorious adulteries.

Virginia worried about how to write "so that we're not all blushing." Vanessa was far more blasé: "I hope you won't mind making us all blush, it won't do any harm." Eventually, Virginia settled on a method that allowed her to begin: "In order that the light of personality may shine through, facts must be manipulated; some must be brightened and others shaded; yet, in the process, they must never lose their integrity."

Virginia began to write Roger's biography in early 1935, during a period of what she called "human emptiness." As the months after his death accumulated, she realized that his absence affected her more deeply than she expected. She was still slogging despondently through *The Years* and felt hopelessly bogged down and unable to finish. And, after a visit to Vita at Sissinghurst, she was saddened by the realization that all their passion had dissipated into formal friendship and that they had nothing in common beyond the memory of past love.

Three years later in 1938, when she was still struggling with both the novel and the biography, she decided to divide her work day in half: mornings for *The Years* and afternoons for *Roger Fry*. She was surprised to find herself shortening the fiction hours to write the biography, but the diversion did not last and it languished. She finished *The Years*, which became a bestseller in both England and the United States; she published *Three Guineas*, which Vita did not like and Maynard Keynes thought silly and badly written; and she was thinking about a new novel (it became *Between the Acts*). In 1939, she went back to the "fearful niggling drudgery"[83] and stuck with it until 1940, when *Roger Fry* became the last work published in her lifetime.

By that time, Julian Bell had died in the Spanish Civil War, Ottoline was dead, Maynard was ailing, and Vita had become a peripheral figure. Only Leonard and Vanessa were there to give Virginia the support she so desperately needed in the final months before her 1941 suicide, and their opinions were divided. Vanessa praised her for bringing to life the Roger she loved; Leonard thought the book dull and lifeless, with too much external quotation and not enough of Virginia's celebrated intuition. Margery Fry expressed "unbounded admiration," which helped lessen the harshness of Leonard's opinion.

The life of Roger Fry has withstood the test of time, justly praised for its qualities and not just because Virginia Woolf wrote it. Today, critics and scholars value it for the ultimate trait she insisted the 20th-century biographer must possess: "he chooses, he synthesizes; in short, he has ceased to be the chronicler, he has become the artist."

68. Virginia Woolf, *The Common Reader*
London: The Hogarth Press, 1925
Private collection

Virginia Woolf, *Autograph letter signed to Augustine Birrell*
July 17, 1929
Private collection

First edition of this selection of her essays, dedicated to Lytton; 1,250 copies were printed. This copy is in the primary binding of white cloth with an illustration by Vanessa, and a gray cloth spine (Kirkpatrick A8a). Of the 21 essays included, "Modern Fiction" and "The Russian Point of View" are two of Woolf's most influential. She added "Miss Ormerod" to her "Lives of the Obscure" essay for the American edition, published later that year by Harcourt. A wonderful association copy, signed in pencil on the front endpaper: *A. Birrell*. With Dadie Rylands's pencil note regarding the marginalia.

With an autograph letter by Virginia, composed on a single leaf of 52 Tavistock Square letterhead, recto covered only, loosely inserted, along with a typed noted signed, "George Rylands / King's College / Cambridge," detailing this volume's provenance; it apparently began life as Birrell's review copy. His son Francis gave it to Raymond Mortimer, who gave it to Bloomsbury collector Robert Reedman on Raymond's 70th birthday in 1972. In 2005, it changed hands again, and is now in another private collection.

While working on her experimental and often controversial fiction, Woolf looked to the essay to earn her a few pounds and a more solid reputation among her peers. How appropriate therefore that this letter, in which she acknowledges the inspiration she derived from reading Birrell's essays, be kept with his copy of her own first volume of critical pieces. She had written in her diary just weeks before, "I must learn to write more succinctly . I am horrified by my own looseness. This is partly that I don't think things out first; partly that I stretch my style to take in crumbs of meaning. But the result is a wobble & diffusity & breathlessness which I detest."[84] Her praise for Birrell in this letter, however, is unqualified:

> I am more than glad that I plucked up courage at Charleston & tried to tell you how much I admire & enjoy your essays. Here they are in this splendid edition, & I have spent the evening foraging among them with a new delight now that they are mine & given me by you. I wish there were more I hadn't read. But I am going to re-read them, & then to put them where they belong next to my Hours in a Library [a collection of Leslie Stephen's essays]. It was very very good of you. Indeed I am almost precipitated by your goodness into the rashness of writing an essay upon Mr. Birrell – making an attempt to find how what [sic] is the particular thing you do so much better than anybody else. That will be a pleasant occupation, – And then there is one other demand I must make on you – to dock me of Woolf & leave Virginia only.
>
> And may I call myself not only admiringly & gratefully but also your affectionate Virginia, as my father's daughter would like to?

The Common Reader received mixed reviews. Muir noted that it shared the high "quality of intelligence" of her novels, "for intelligence works by the same means, whatever theme may confront it. She has the informed enthusiasm which criticism should never lack, but which is tending to disappear from it; her judgments have admirable breadth." Never one to praise unequivocally, he found her lacking a crucial quality – "the power of wide and illuminating generalization" – but admitted that she "holds the scales even, as she does between her characters in *Night and Day*; she uses her sensibility as she used it in *Jacob's Room* and *Mrs. Dalloway*. It is the same mind, and we never doubt its competence to deal with anything which it fixes upon."[85] The following month she surveyed other reviews: "The Lit. Sup. had close on 2 columns sober & sensible praise – neither one thing nor the other – my fate in the Times. And Goldie [Goldsworthy Lowes Dickinson] writes that he thinks 'this is the best criticism in English – humorous, witty & profound.' – My fate is to be treated to all extremes & all mediocrities."

69. Virginia Woolf, *The Common Reader. Second Series*
London: The Hogarth Press, 1932
Private collection

First edition; 3,200 copies (Kirkpatrick A18a). The dust-jackets for both volumes were designed by Vanessa. Most of the articles had previously appeared in the *TLS*, the *Nation*, *Vogue*, the *Yale Review*, *Figaro*, and other periodicals, and cover subjects from the Elizabethans through the Romantics, concluding with Woolf's essay, "How Should One Read a Book?"

A presentation copy, inscribed on the front endpaper to the third of Lytton's five sisters, Philippa: *Pippa with love from Virginia*. In 1907, an active suffragist ten years' Virginia's senior, Pippa organized the first significant women's rights procession through London on behalf of the London Society of Women's Suffrage. She remained secretary of that organization – renamed the National Society for Women's Service – until 1951. Though she and Virginia, enjoying significantly different lifestyles, were not intimate, they shared a mutual, if conditional, affection and respect that is apparent in Virginia's diaries and letters. In February 1918, she examined Pippa's worldview in her journal, with a subtle mix of concern and admiration:

> Pippa has faded curiously; looks older, & more worn. She spoke of old days of parties, H. B. Smith, George Duckworth, Jack Hills & Christmases at Corby. She thinks that still the way to live; those people so "civilised" compared with our cropheads. But now she has no time for society; does suffrage, which will turn now into a campaign for equality, by day & night. It struck me that age consists not in having a different point of view, but in having the same point of view, faded.

She includes in the entry Pippa's comments on herself:

> "Mercifully," she said, "there are people like you who keep out of it. It's most important that there should be people like you. That is so long as you've got or earned economic independence. That's essential."

Though they channeled their energies into very different activities – Virginia into writing, and Pippa into politics – each would ultimately forward the cause of women's equality. In 1938, after reading the advance copy of *Three Guineas* Virginia had sent her, Pippa wrote in support: "She is enthusiastic," Virginia confided in her diary, "So this is the last load off my mind – which weighed it rather heavy, for I felt if I had written all that & it was not to her liking I should have to brace myself pretty severely in my own private esteem. But she says it's the very thing for which they have panted..."[86]

70. Virginia Woolf, *Mr. Bennett and Mrs. Brown*
London: The Hogarth Press, 1924
Private collection

Arnold Bennett, *Books and Persons*
Corrected typescript, December 1926
Mortimer Rare Book Room, Smith College

First separate edition of this essay first published in the "Literary Review" of the *New York Evening Post*, and reprinted in *Nation & Athenaeum* and *Living Age*. It also provided the basis for her influential essay, "Character in Fiction." 1,000 copies were printed, and 1,000 more four years later (Woolmer 54). Together with Bennett's manuscript attack on literary Modernism (in his review of *The Common Reader*, *Mrs. Dalloway*, and *Jacob's Room*, which appeared in the *Evening Standard* on December 2, 1926).

"To disagree about character is to differ in the depths of the being...." Virginia revised and expanded her incendiary response to Bennett's review – from its first incarnation in *The New York Evening Post* in November 1923, for presentation to the Heretics society at Cambridge in May 1924, and further revised it for this publication as part of the Hogarth Essays series. Bennett's essay, "Is the Novel Decaying?," appeared in *Cassell's Weekly* in March 1923. It engendered a spirited debate on the concept of "character-creation in fiction," in which Virginia broke down and swept away Bennett, Wells, and Galsworthy, and invited Forster, Lawrence, Strachey, Joyce, and Eliot to pave the road to "one of the great ages of English literature."

Bennett declared that Woolf and her generation are crippled by a failure to attend to the individual, and by a desire for "cleverness, which is perhaps the lowest of all artistic qualities . I have seldom read a cleverer book than Virginia Woolf's *Jacob's Room*, a novel which has made a great stir in a small world. It is packed and bursting with originality, and it is exquisitely written. But the characters do not vitally survive in the mind because the author has been obsessed by details of originality and cleverness."

Virginia had challenged Bennett on his "point of view" as early as 1917, and in "Mr. Bennett and Mrs. Brown" – in which "Mrs. Brown" is a hypothetical character in search of definition – blamed him directly for the gradual but certain "evaporation" of "character-making power" in the novel. "Mr. Bennett blames the Georgians," but Woolf blames Bennett, calling his "the fatal age, the age which is just breaking off from our own, the age when character disappeared or was mysteriously engulfed." The difference between the novels of the Edwardians, as represented by Wells, Galsworthy, and Bennett, and of the Georgians, she writes, is one of purpose: "[I]t seems to be that to go to these men and ask them to teach you how to write a novel – how to create characters that are real – is precisely like going to a bootmaker and asking him to teach you how to make a watch . There are seasons when it is more important to have boots than to have watches," but the result is that "they leave one with so strange a feeling of incompleteness and dissatisfaction. In order to complete them it seems necessary to do something – to join a society, or, more desperately, to write a cheque." Her conclusion is that "the Edwardians were never interested in character in itself; or in the book in itself. They were interested in something outside."

She champions her generation, but is not defensive, claiming they are doing the best they can without the aid of contemporary models. "[W]e hear all round us, in poems and novels and biographies, even in newspaper articles and essays, the sound of breaking and falling, crashing and destruction," as "the strong are led to destroy the very foundations and rule of literary society. Signs of this are everywhere apparent. Grammar is violated; syntax disintegrated . . . we must reconcile ourselves to a season of failures and fragments."

71. Virginia Woolf, *Autograph letter signed to a Mr. Castle*

November 18, 1915
Private collection

Virginia writes to an old acquaintance: she mentioned Adrian's marriage – "I daresay you have heard" – sends well wishes from Leonard, and writes of her own personal circumstances: "It was extremely kind of you to write to me about *The Voyage Out*, & I have taken a long time to answer, but I have been ill, & not allowed to write letters even."

She devotes the rest of the letter to *The Voyage Out*, to discussing issues of structure – the importance of Rachel's death – and character, exploring the ways in which she feels she failed, and with more than a hint of the theories she would work out more fully in *Mr. Bennett and Mrs. Brown*:

> I am very glad that the characters seemed to you vivid (& the scenery which I rather impudently made up out of my head). I thought that the main fault of the book was that I brought in too many different people to be able, in that space, to make them interesting to the reader . I think the scheme was too ambitious for an inexperienced novelist, & I am the more glad that you found so much to like.

72. Virginia Woolf, *"Reviewing"*

Corrected typescript, 1939
Mortimer Rare Book Room, Smith College

Corrected typescript of her essay of which Leonard published over 5,000 copies. In it, Virginia tackles the negative impact of reviewers, a subject with which she had had much first-hand experience.

73. Raymond Mortimer, *The Bloomsbury Group*

New York: Harcourt, Brace and Company, ca. 1928
Private collection

This promotional pamphlet, "specially bound for presentation," contains a reprint of Raymond Mortimer's essay "the Bloomsbury Group" from *The Dial* (February 1928), with brief biographical sketches of Clive, Lytton, and Virginia ("In her novels she is a pioneer whose full importance cannot even yet be gauged"). Also printed are promotional blurbs on their recently published titles, *Civilization*, *Orlando*, and *Elizabeth and Essex*.

74. Virginia Woolf, *Letter to a Young Poet*
Manuscript, 1931
The Morgan Library and Museum

Virginia's manuscript notebook containing, among other pieces, her heavily revised manuscript draft for this essay addressed to John Lehmann but published in the June 1932 issue of *The Yale Review* and later that year as part of the Hogarth Press Letters. In it, she investigates the faults and foibles of modern poetry. In *A Letter to Mrs. Virginia Woolf*, published as Number 12 of The Hogarth Letters that October, Peter Quennell responded on behalf of his generation to Virginia's criticism. Under pressure from a disgruntled Lehmann, she later recanted much of this letter: "[T]he fact is I'm not at all satisfied with the Letter, and would like to tear up, or entirely re-write. It is a bad form for criticism, because it seems to invite archness and playfulness, and when one has done being playful the times up and there's no room for more. However the B.B.C. have caught on to the idea and want to have a series of letters to unknown Listeners in the autumn." [87]

75. Virginia Woolf, *Three typed letters signed to Helen McAfee,* Yale Review
March 16, 1926, July 7, 1930, January 17, 1932
Private collection

Three letters Virginia wrote over the course of six years. Her relationship with the *Yale Review* began through McAfee. In 1926 Virginia thanks her for a letter promising a copy of the *Review* in which Forster's review of her work appears, and asks if she may purchase a pair of additional copies. She called Forster's essay, which she read in manuscript, "a beautiful piece of criticism," though she admits she may not be completely impartial. As a postscript she adds, "It would give me much pleasure to send you an article some time, if you would tell me what sort of thing you suits you [sic]. At present, I have only criticism" – which she crossed out, writing in "critical articles" above – to offer. "How Should One Read a Book?" appeared in the *Yale Review* that October and "Street Haunting: A London Adventure" the following year.

In 1930 Virginia writes in thanks for a check – for her article on Augustine Birrell. She writes of the pattern her life has taken – "we are mainly down here [i.e., at Rodmell] at the present time, tempted by our garden, though we have generally to come up for a day or two to look after the Hogarth Press" – and then again offers her work:

> The only thing I have written that might interest you – as you ask about future work – is an introductory letter to a little book of working womens [sic] memoirs that we are publishing in the au-

tumn. It is about 5,000 words in length, and consists really of my recollections of various co-coperative [sic] congresses and reflections upon working women, in the form of a letter to Miss Llewellyn Davies who used to be the head of the Womens Guild.

That piece appeared in the *Yale Review* in September.

Two years after that, Virginia is still addressing her editor as "Miss McAfee." In January 1932 – the month in which McAfee published her "Oxford Street Tide" – she writes of the press on *The Waves,* apparently in response to McAfee's own remarks:

> ... people have been very kind, but they have been puzzled, many of them. And as I think I told you about Orlando, the author is the last person to know what she meant . I certainly did not mean, as some critics say, to write a book about the inside of the mind solely. I think I meant on the contrary to be abstract and objective. I left out much detail for that reason. I did not want them to be characters in the ordinary sense of the word. I think I wanted to epitomise experience, not to care for the individual type. But as I say, one works half consciously – one has to go to one's critics for the outside view. Yours was one of those that most interested me.

Virginia concludes, again, with material available for publication; references a "Mr. Skinner"; and requests the purchase of a Yale Shakespeare, which she has been told is "far the best." Virginia published three more times in the *Yale Review* in her lifetime; an additional essay was published nearly four decades after her death.

VIII. Her Feminism
Orlando, A Room of One's Own, and *Three Guineas*

Vita Sackville-West as Orlando
1928

The Fall of a Flower Mark Hussey

In the fall of 1928, three weeks before the publication of *Orlando*, her fantastic "biography" of Vita Sackville-West, Virginia Woolf traveled to France with her lover. Vita noted in the diary she kept of their trip that on the day they left Virginia and her husband "had had a small & sudden row that morning about her going abroad with me."[88] Once in France, Virginia was continually anxious about letters from Leonard, eventually sending him a telegram from Avallon: "No letters anxious wire Hotel de la Poste Vézelay."[89]

At Vézelay, where they arrived on September 27, they did not go into the great Church of the Magdalen. Vita wrote to Virginia a few days after their return to England that she had just read Walter Pater's essay about the church: "I say, that narthex I kept worrying about is one of the glories of France, it seems. And we never saw it."[90] Another Pater had come up in their conversations in France, however: Clara, Walter's sister, from whom Virginia had as a teenager taken lessons in Greek and Intermediate Latin.

At the beginning of 1928 Woolf sold a short story to the New York magazine *Forum*, the inspiration for which is recorded in a diary entry she made as she finished writing *To the Lighthouse*: "As usual, side stories are sprouting in great variety as I wind this up: a book of characters; the whole string being pulled out from some simple sentence, like Clara Pater's, 'Don't you find that Barker's pins have no points to them?'"[91] Woolf wrote to Vita, "I've just written, or re-written, a nice little story about Sapphism, for the Americans."[92] "'Slater's Pins Have No Points'" netted her 60, she told Vita – a "little Sapphist story of which the Editor has not seen the point, though he's been looking for it in the Adirondacks."[93]

The "point" of that little story, which begins with a flower that falls to the floor, having become unpinned from a dress, might well have been something Woolf felt she ought to obscure. Just before setting off for France, she had written to Vita about their shared outrage over the suppression by the Home Secretary of Radclyffe Hall's clumsy lesbian novel *The Well of Loneliness*. Hall was not an easy person to champion, insisting on drawing up her own letter for her principled supporters to sign. "So," Virginia told Vita, "nothing could be done, except indeed one rather comic little letter written by Morgan Forster, which he asked me to sign: and now it appears that I, the mouthpiece of Sapphism, write letters from the Reform Club."[94]

In 1943, after Virginia's death, Leonard included the story in the collection *A Haunted House* under the full title she had given it in typescript, "Moments of Being: 'Slater's Pins Have No Points'." The story concerns a piano student, Fanny Wilmot, who is infatuated with her teacher, Julia Craye, sister of a "famous archaeologist." A rose has fallen from Fanny's dress, occasioning a version of the remark that Woolf recalled as having been made by Clara Pater. While she hunts on the floor for her pin, Fanny reveals intense feelings for Miss Craye, thinking in particular about how her teacher has preserved her independence by resisting marriage: "They're ogres," she had said one evening, half laughing, when another pupil, a girl lately married, suddenly bethinking her that she would miss her husband, had rushed off in haste.[95]

The story's penultimate paragraph, in which Fanny is either kissed or has a vision of being kissed by Miss Craye, differs in the two published versions. In *Forum*, it read:

> She saw Julia open her arms; saw her blaze; saw her kindle. Out of the night she burnt like a dead white star. Julia kissed her. Julia possessed her.[96]

But in the typescript that Leonard followed in 1943 we find this:

> Julia blazed. Julia kindled. Out of the night she burnt like a dead white star. Julia opened her arms. Julia kissed her on the lips. Julia possessed it.

What "it" is that Julia possessed can be understood from earlier in the story where Miss Craye has retrieved the flower (now, mysteriously, a carnation)[97] from the floor and "crushed it voluptuously" in her hands. Yet, "this crush and grasp of the finger was combined with a perpetual frustration. So it was even now with the carnation. She had her hands on it; she pressed it; but she did not possess it, enjoy it, not entirely and altogether."[98]

At breakfast on the third day of their holiday, Vita and Virginia had a "heated argument about men & women. V. is curiously feminist," Vita remarked; "She dislikes the possessiveness and love of domination in men. In fact she dislikes the quality of masculinity. Says that women stimulate her imagination, by their grace & their art of life."[99] This was no lightly held opinion of Woolf's. She reiterated it in a letter to Ethel Smyth in 1930: "Women alone stir my imagination."[100] Indeed, Virginia's love of women was a theme of her conversations with Vita in France. On the day they left Vézelay they stopped at a tea-shop and browsed an *antiquaire* where Virginia bought a looking-glass. Later, Vita wrote, "V. told me the history of her early loves,—Madge Symon[d]s, who is Sally in *Mrs Dalloway*."[101]

At Vézelay they had had an experience that affected Vita very deeply, so much that she recalled it five years later in a letter to Virginia:

> Oh I've got so much to say to you – but it takes hours – I mean, the sort of things I want to say to you require prolonged intimacy before they can squeeze themselves out. [...] Do you remember a night in Burgundy? [. .] when I came along the dark passage to your room in a thunderstorm and we lay talking about whether we were frightened of death or not? That is the sort of occasion on which the things I want to say to you, – and to you only, – get said.[102]

In her diary at the time Vita had written:

> In the middle of the night I was woken up by a thunderstorm. Went along to V's room thinking she might be frightened. We talked about science & religion for an hour – and the ultimate principle – and then as the storm had gone over I left her to go to sleep again.[103]

The next day, Virginia too referred to the storm in a letter to Leonard, adding vaguely: "we all crouched in our beds in fear."[104] And maybe in France, or maybe back in England, either at the end of September 1928 or perhaps later, Vita sketched rapidly a poem that sheds light on the conversations she and Virginia had, away from their husbands, in a hotel in Burgundy, conversations about the love of women for women, about Pater's sister, about the bonds of marriage, and about the "ultimate principle." This sketch of a poem offers a slight but provocative difference from the narrative as we have seen it recorded by Virginia and Vita thus far: "she came into my room."

The month after their return from France, Vita accompanied Virginia to Cambridge where she gave the first of the two lectures from which derive *A Room of One's Own*. In that great feminist essay Woolf writes that fiction "is like a spider's web, attached ever so lightly perhaps, but still attached to life at all four corners." Even the most sublime works of art "are not spun in mid-air by incorporeal creatures, but are the work of suffering human beings, and are attached to grossly material things, like health and money and the houses we live in."[105] From the dispersed and fragmentary records of lived experience and of creativity that now belong to libraries or that are in private hands we continue to build up images that remain forever incomplete of that life to which fiction is attached. "Pater's Sister" – or "The Pin & the Thunderstorm" – adds a little more to our understanding of the relationship Vita and Virginia shared. It helps us to understand why Vita returned once more to the memory of their trip to France when she wrote about Virginia's published diary in 1954, and specifically to the memory of "a conversation I once had with her during a nocturnal thunderstorm on a Burgundian hill-top, when she was, I surmise, too much frightened to go to bed, and physical fear released the founts of spiritual horror."[106]

Reading *A Writer's Diary* Vita's memory may have been stimulated by what Woolf calls in *The Waves* "a little language such as lovers use."[107] Just two months after thinking she might spin a story out of the remark about pins with no points she recalled Clara Pater having made, Woolf began to think about the novel many regard as her masterpiece, *The Waves*. In setting down the first intimations of that work she used a phrase that would have resonated uniquely for Vita Sackville-West:

> Yet I am now and then haunted by some semi-mystic very profound life of a woman, which shall all be told on one occasion; and time shall be utterly obliterated; future shall somehow blossom out of the past. One incident – say the fall of a flower – might contain it.[108]

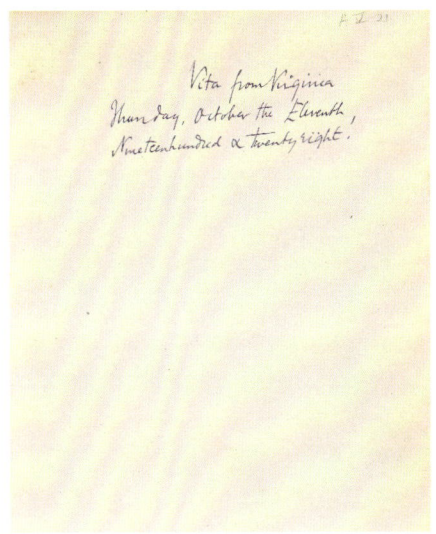
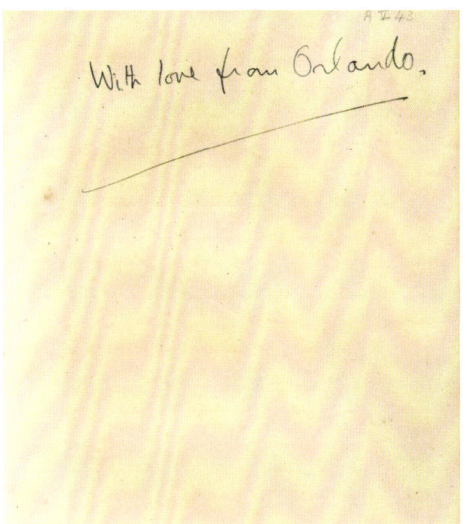

76. Virginia Woolf, *Orlando*
    London: The Hogarth Press, 1928
    Private collection

Virginia Woolf, *Orlando*
    London: The Hogarth Press, 1928
    Private collection

First English editions, issued a matter of days after the October 2 release of the Crosby Gaige edition in New York; 5,080 copies, followed by an additional 3,000 copies later that month and a further 3,000 copies in January of 1929 (Kirkpatrick A11b, Woolmer 185).

    The first is the dedication copy, inscribed to Vita enthusiastically on publication day: *Vita from Virginia / Thursday, October the Eleventh, Nineteenhundred & twenty-eight!*

    The volume was later specially bound, with the upper panel of the dust-jacket bound-in, and with a humorous clipping affixed to the binder's front endpaper, misidentifying the author of the book as Rebecca West and misspelling Vita's married name. The Nicolsons, remembered today largely for their home Sissinghurst, arguably England's most famous garden, had a library as moist as a greenhouse, and this volume is, therefore, foxed. It bears a discreet pencil notation that most likely represents the family's library code: "A V 41." With a letter by Nigel Nicolson discussing the provenance of the first edition copy:

> It was sent to my mother, Vita Sackville-West, on the day of publication, October 11th 1928, the date inscribed by the author on the fly-leaf, and repeated on page 295, the last words of the book. It was in this copy that Vita read the book for the first time, having been kept in ignorance of its contents, although she is the subject and dedicatee of the novel, and the photographs appearing opposite pp. 144, 224 and 288 are of her. The portrait opposite p. 240 is at Sissinghurst, the others at Knole.

The final paragraph of the book reads, "And the twelfth stroke of midnight sounded; the twelfth stroke of midnight, Thursday, the eleventh of October, Nineteen hundred and Twenty Eight." Nigel further states that the clipping on the binder's leaf was in fact "inserted by Virginia Woolf as a joke."

The second copy is inscribed by Vita, as "Orlando," to her husband, Harold Nicolson: *With love from Orlando.* Signed by Vita on the front pastedown, *V.N. / Long Barn*. With the library note in pencil, "A V 43."

In *Orlando* Woolf questions traditional notions of gender and genre, pushing the boundaries of sexual politics while parodying centuries of English literary and political forms. Essentially, *Orlando* is a fictional biography, beginning with Orlando's adolescence in 17th-century England and ending in 1928 – the year the book was published – and includes a spontaneous sex-change in which Orlando becomes Lady Orlando. Readers meet Orlando at the start of his 400-year journey in the attic of his family home, and follow him while he attends to the Queen, falls in love, wakes up one morning as a woman, travels to London, and struggles while writing a long play titled "The Oak Tree."

These stylistic feats, however, take a back seat to the autobiographical elements of the novel, much of which is derived from Vita's life and from her relationship with Virginia.

Virginia had written to Vita, her close friend before and after their love affair, for approval of the project: " suppose Orlando turns out to be Vita; and it's all about you and the lusts of your flesh and the lure of your mind ... Shall you mind? Say yes, or no." Vita was completely willing, "thrilled and terrified" by the prospect, and supplied several photographs as well as reproductions of four paintings from her home. (The frontispiece portrait of Orlando as a boy, for example, is Vita's cousin Eddy Sackville.) Virginia drew upon her relationship with Vita and her knowledge of the Sackville-West ancestry to shape the character of Orlando and his history, using Vita's *Knole and the Sackvilles* in imagining Orlando's estate, and her poem "The Land" in composing his play, "The Oak Tree." Most poignant is Orlando's transformation from man to woman: As a woman, Orlando would not be able to inherit her beloved ancestral home, just as in reality Vita could never, according to the laws of entail, inherit Knole. After the book's release, Vita wrote that she was "completely dazzled, bewitched, enchanted, under a spell," and called it "the loveliest, wisest, *richest* book that I have ever read ." Of course: it was a portrait of her life, both as it was and as it might have been, across time and gender. But it was also about Virginia herself. The subject of *Orlando* is ostensibly Vita, but the autobiographical strains have not been overlooked. Despite mixed reviews – which ranged from negative to glowing to simply confused – Virginia's homage to androgyny and to Vita was a best-seller; during the first six months 8,104 copies were sold in England and 13,301 in the States.

Virginia and Vita met in 1922 and acknowledged an immediate and mutual chemistry. Each treated their subsequent love affair in her writing in myriad ways. Their relationship inspired Vita's *Seducers in Equador* (1924), which was written for Virginia and published, as were many of Vita's subsequent efforts, by the Woolfs at the Hogarth Press. Virginia's *Orlando* (1928) was the most public and scandalous declaration of their love. In turn, Vita composed private, unpublished – perhaps even unsent – love poems to Virginia (in 1925 and 1928). In *All Passion Spent* (1931) she gives a public and intellectual nod to Woolf's *A Room of One's Own*, which Vita heard Virginia recite in the form of Cambridge lectures.

Vita wrote to Virginia just a few days before their first meeting, with a pastoral poem, *Sissinghurst*, which the Hogarth Press would publish the following year; Rhein describes it as "one of the most perfectly designed and executed of all the hand printed books." The commercial side of the Press published thirteen books for Vita in all, including a novel, several travel books, a biography of her grandmother, and, of course, poetry.

Virginia once said that Vita had taught her much and provided her with a contentment she had never known. When she disappeared in March 1941, both Leonard and Virginia's sister Vanessa wrote frequently and repeatedly to Vita as hope of her survival waned and her body was eventually discovered; Vanessa wrote of Vita as "the person Virginia loved most I think outside her own family." Vita's memorial poem to Virginia appeared in *The Observer* on April 6, 1941.

77. (Geddes) Paul Hyslop, *Eddy Sackville*

Knole, 1927
Courtesy Abbott and Holder Ltd.

Photo of Vita's cousin Eddy taken the year before publication of *Orlando*, a book in which he is wryly thanked in the preface, with so many others, for his assistance. Among other services he posed for one of the photographs in the book. Virginia was inspired to write *Orlando* as a way to rewrite Vita's life by allowing her to inherit her ancestral home, Knole. Because of the laws of primogeniture, her brother would inherit the estate upon their father's passing, in 1928. Knole passed to Eddy in 1962, coincidentally the year Vita died. Eddy, too, was a Hogarth Press author, if a minor one. The Woolfs published him twice: *Apology of Arthur Rimbaud: A Dialogue* in 1927 (Hogarth Essays Second Series number 7) and the translation he prepared with Vita of Rilke's *Duineser Elegien* in 1931.

78. Virginia Woolf, *Orlando*

Corrected page proofs
June 9–July 22, 1928
Mortimer Rare Book Room, Smith College

Virginia's heavily corrected proofs to the first edition of *Orlando*, stamped throughout by printers H & R Clarke with dates ranging from June 9 through July 22, 1928, stamped occasional "first proof," and docketed in a setter's hand, here and there, "marked proof."

Virginia began writing *Orlando* in earnest in 1927 and completed her first draft in March 1928, after which she awaited proofs to which she would make unrestrained revisions. In these page proofs, issued to Virginia in June 1928, she makes hundreds of substantial textual refinements, adding, deleting, and adjusting hundreds of lines throughout, finalizing her copyright, struggling with the dedication, and refining language. In some instances she merely rewords extant passages; in others, as in a discussion of "men of genius," like "Addison, Swift, Pope," she provides two versions of a summarizing statement: "yet after all they were not much different from other people."

She inscribed these proof sheets to her publisher, likely less as a formal presentation and more as simple matter of forwarding them: *Corrected Proofs For Mr. Gaige.*

79. Vita Sackville-West, *"Your darkened windows numb my darkened heart"*
Manuscript, ca. August 1925
Private collection

Vita Sackville-West, *"The Pin and the Thunderstorm"*
Manuscript, ca. 1928
Private collection

The first poem, three stanzas unsigned, untitled, and undated, describes the night Vita secretly stood looking down at Virginia's house from a distance and a visit they made to Knole; it reads in full:

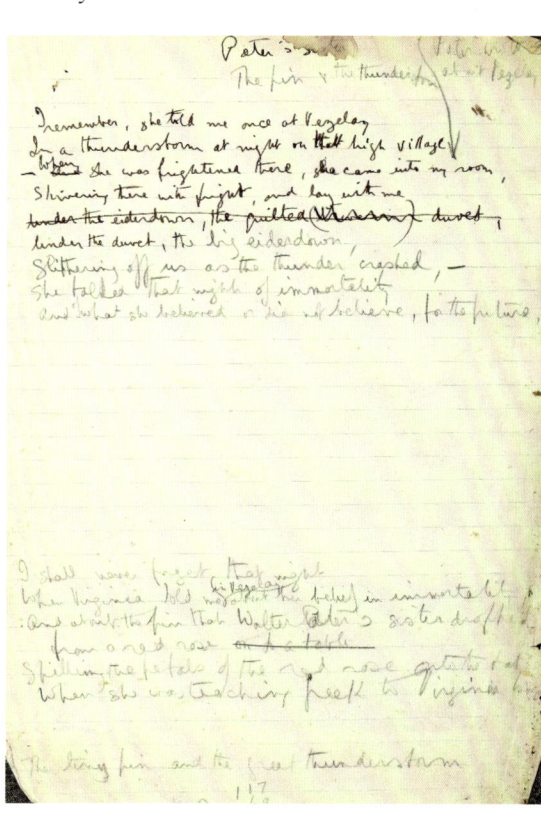

Your darkened windows numb my darkened heart.
I look in vain across the sable night,
And rage against your separate life apart
Which robs me even of a casement light.

Where are you gone? Who seeing? Where, or where,
Loved stranger, daily but elusive friend,
Gone with the dusk in other lives to share,
Leaving me but to guess and apprehend?

—Only, tonight my heart may triumph keep:
Your golden casement suffers its eclipse,
But it was I who dimmed your lights to sleep
And left you with my kiss upon your lips.

The imagery and tone of these quatrains is clearly echoed in Vita's letter to Virginia on August 25, 1925:

> Last Friday at midnight I stood on top of your Downs, and, looking down over various lumps of blackness, tried to guess which valley contained Rodmell and you asleep therein. And now comes your letter, making me think that on the contrary you were probably awake and in pain. But

knowing nothing of that at the time, I reluctantly recovered my dogs who had been galloping madly across the Downs, climbed into the motor, and drove on along deserted roads and through the sleeping villages of Sussex and Kent, with the secret knowledge in my own mind that I had paid you a visit of which you knew nothing – more romantic, if less satisfying, than a cup of tea to which Leonard had bidden me on Saturday....

The second manuscript, composed in a frantic hand, in ink and pencil, with revisions, is about a night spent in a hotel room in France with Virginia in 1928. Titled in ink, "Pater's Sister," and then in pencil, "The Pin & the Thunderstorm," it reads,

> I remember, she told me once at Vezelay
> In a thunderstorm at night on that high village
> When she was frightened there, she came into my room,
> [insertion, possibly here:] Pater wrote about Vezelay,
> Shivering there with fright, and lay with me
> ~~Under the eiderdown, the quilted duvet~~
> Under the duvet, the big eiderdown,
> Glittering off us as the thunder crashed, –
> She talked that night of immortality
> And what she believed or did not believe, for the future,
>
> [ten blank lines]
>
> I shall never forget that night
> When Virginia told me in Vezelay about her belief in immortality
> And about the pin that Walter Pater's sister dropped
> From a red rose ~~on to a table~~
> Spilling the petals of the red rose onto the table
> When she was teaching Greek to Virginia
>
> [two blank lines]
>
> The tiny pin and the great thunderstorm.

Once Vita and Harold had settled into their marriage, they shared a tacit understanding about their sexual independence. Vita embarked on a short-lived affair with Geoffrey Scott, but she left her only heterosexual lover for Virginia, whom she had first met through Clive Bell at the end of 1922. Virginia recalled the introduction: "the lovely aristocratic Sackville-West last night at Clive's. Not much to my severer taste with all the supple ease of the aristocracy, but not the wit of the artist. She writes 15 pages a day – has finished another book – publishes with Heinemann – knows everyone – but could I ever know her?"

In 1925, Harold was posted as Councellor to the British Legation in Teheran for a term of 18 months. Vita, too interested in maintaining her independence to commit herself as a full-time diplomat's wife in Persia, made periodic visits. Her impressions of such exotic landscapes, mysterious people, and strange ways of life appeared in correspondence, diary entries, and eventually in two books. At home, Virginia was occupying more of Vita's time and thoughts. They spent intimate nights together at

Monk's House, Virginia's home, and at Long Barn. Virginia took Vita to Charleston Farmhouse to visit Vanessa and Clive. In a letter to Harold, Vita described it as "a soul-friendship. Very good for me and good for her too."

Vita took Virginia to Knole for the first time in January 1927. The vision of Vita, exotically attired in Turkish dress as she stalked the halls, caught fire in Virginia's mind, and engendered the conception of *Orlando*, a paean to Vita and her relationship to Knole that Vita's son Nigel later described as "the longest and most charming love letter in literature." The following month, Vita was off to meet Harold in Persia for another month of arduous travel. When they returned to England at the end of April, they resolved that Harold would resign from diplomatic service, and invited South African poet Roy Campbell, and his wife Mary, to move into the gardener's cottage at Long Barn. It was not long before their good intentions were uprooted. Harold was forced to accept the position of Councillor in the British Embassy in Berlin. Vita began a volatile affair with Mary, the stress of which inspired her to write a series of eleven sonnets. Meanwhile, Virginia was deep into *Orlando,* requesting Vita to pose for photographs that would be used to illustrate the book.

Throughout the 1930s, while the world grew increasingly unsettled, Vita's friendship with Virginia continued to be a great source of comfort and inspiration. Gas shortages curtailed regular visits, but on occasion Vita was able to travel to the Woolfs' home, and treated them to scarce and rationed commodities such as Sissinghurst-produced butter and knitting wool.

80. Virginia Woolf, *A Room of One's Own*
London: The Hogarth Press, 1929
Private collection

First English edition, trade issue, in the dust-jacket designed by Vanessa; 3,040 copies were printed; an edition of 492 numbered copies signed by Woolf was published simultaneously in New York by The Fountain Press, distributed in London by the Hogarth Press and in New York by Random House (Kirkpatrick A12b, Woolmer 215B). Hussey reports that over 22,000 copies were sold in the first six months; Penguin issued a paperback in 1945.

With Dadie Rylands's bookplate on the front pastedown, his pencil note on the front endpaper, *First edition*, and his explanation of his participation in the text beneath: *The luncheon on page 16 took place in my rooms. GMR.* On pages 16 and following, Woolf describes in satisfying detail the courses served at the luncheon, defying the "novelist's convention not to mention soup and salmon and ducklings, as if soup and salmon and ducklings were of no importance whatsoever, as if nobody ever smoked a cigar or drank a glass of wine." She immortalizes Dadie's luncheon – without mentioning him by name –by describing the rare comfort she felt at this particular gathering: "No need to hurry. No need to sparkle. No need to be anybody but oneself ... how good life seemed, how sweet its rewards, how trivial this grudge or that grievance, how admirable friendship and the society of one's kind...." A loosely inserted document lists a few of the coterie present at the luncheon on October 21, 1928, quoting a letter from Maynard Keynes: "I've just come away from a lunch at Dadie's with Lytton, Leonard, Virginia, Vanessa, Julian and Angelica! It was very pleasant – Virginia had been reading a paper last night to the young ladies at Newnham whom she finds beautiful, charming and intelligent! So there !"

Virginia indeed composed *A Room of One's Own* after lecture visits to Newnham and Girton, the two women's colleges in Cambridge, in the fall of 1928. On October 20 she had traveled with Leonard, Vanessa, and Angelica Bell to deliver a talk to the students of Newnham, of which Lytton's sister Pernel was the principal. She stayed with Pernel, and lunched in Dadie's rooms with Lytton, Maynard, and the others. The following week she went to Cambridge with Vita to give a talk at Girton, and took that opportunity to visit Julian in his rooms. Upon returning home she reported on her audience: "Starved but valiant young women – that's my impression. Intelligent, eager, poor; and destined to become schoolmistresses in shoals. I blandly told them to drink wine and have a room of their own. Why should all the splendour, all the luxury of life be lavished on the Julians and the Francises, and none on the [Elizabeth] Phares & the [Margaret Ellen] Thomases?" She then set out to work this into publishable form, examining the differences in educational experiences allotted women and men, and the impact of these experiences on women's writing.

81. Virginia Woolf, *A Room of One's Own*
London: The Hogarth Press, 1929
Private collection

First edition, trade issue. A stellar association copy, tying three prominent literary women of Paris to the text. Inscribed on the front endpaper by Oscar Wilde's niece Dolly Wilde to Natalie Clifford Barney: *For Natalie, from her own room. Dolly. / Paris 1929*. With Sylvia Beach's bookplate on the front pastedown: "Ex-Libris Shakespeare and Company / Sylvia Beach / Paris." After the Woolfs, unable to find a capable and willing printer, turned down the manuscript of Joyce's *Ulysses*, Beach of course undertook the monumental project.

The conversational style and seductive tone of *A Room of One's Own* have, as a background, Virginia's relationship with Vita. A less benign backdrop is the trial, in the previous year, of Radclyffe Hall's *The Well of Loneliness*, to which Woolf makes a significant allusion. Both Virginia and Vita had rallied to its defense[109], albeit not on literary grounds. Whatever the faults of Radclyffe Hall's novel, it remains interesting for its barely disguised portrait of Natalie Clifford Barney as Valerie Seymour, a wealthy American expatriate in Paris who is not only beautiful, charming, witty, and popular but entirely comfortable with her lesbianism. She is "a kind of pioneer who would probably go down in history... her love affairs would fill quite three volumes [and] all intelligent people realized that she was a creature apart."

A version of Virginia's dream of female community found form in Barney's lesbian salon. Djuna Barnes's *Ladies Almanack*, also published in 1928, celebrated Barney's circle, portraying Barney as Evangeline Musset and Dolly Wilde as Doll Furious. Barney and Wilde met in 1927, and Dolly would become Barney's most vivid love of that decade and the next. She not only bore a striking resemblance to her uncle Oscar but also, according to Barney's biographer, George Wickes, "had the same extravagant gifts and failings, the indolence, the personal magnetism and that breathtaking effortless wit." Some of these characteristics found memorial in a cancelled episode of F. Scott Fitzgerald's *Tender Is the Night* (1934).

"She never had enough money or what Virginia Woolf meant by a Room of Her Own," wrote Dolly's

biographer, Joan Schenkar. "Without the *mise en scène* of the Barney salon ... the eccentric gifts and killing wit of someone like Dolly Wilde would have vanished into anecdote, or into footnote, or into the unmarked, crossroads grave Virginia Woolf reserved for Shakespeare's brilliant, imaginary, suicide sister in *A Room of One's Own*, a work whose subject uncannily suggests some of the trials of Dolly's own life." Schenkar's footnote to that sentence goes further: "It would be interesting to know if Virginia Woolf, who met and was amused by Dolly, might have had Dolly in mind while she was writing *A Room of One's Own*. The parallels are disconcerting."

Dolly and Barney's letters reveal their discussion of many writers but in particular Virginia, with whom they both closely identified. "I am to dine with Virginia one day next week – but I dread the ordeal and she will never know what marginal notes of understanding mark every page of her books in my library," wrote Dolly to Barney. The letter that followed drew a fine portrait of Virginia and mentioned how "suddenly I say something that makes her laugh and the curtain of her eye-lids are [sic] raised and we talk together, flippantly delightfully. I had once been told one must never mention her books and as we threaded byways of humour I thought of your letters so much. I saw her, too, all the time as such a pretty little girl in a big hat, and *Kew Gardens* with the governess planting a kiss on the back of her neck – do you remember? – which was the parent of all the kisses in her life." After dinner, they went to see a performance of *Hamlet* and Dolly had to turn her head away when she caught Virginia yawning, "as if I had caught God in a domestic moment of relaxation."

82. George Sand, *Histoire de ma Vie*

Paris, Michel Lévy, 1856
Private collection

Autograph letters signed to Susie Tweedsmuir, August 1, 1938, August 3, 1939

Private collection

Second edition of Sand's memoir (the first was issued in 1854-55), 20 volumes in ten, each covered and labeled by Virginia and sent to her friend Susan Buchan. Together with two lengthy and substantive autograph letters, one unpublished.

Susan Buchan (née Grosvenor) and Virginia knew each other as children and rekindled their friendship in later years after "Susie" married the writer John Buchan (today best known for *The 39 Steps*), who became Lord Tweedsmuir when he was named Governor General of Canada in 1935. The two shared a friend in Elizabeth Bowen, to whom Susie confided, long after Virginia's death, that she numbered this set of George Sand among her "most treasured possessions." In her memoir, Susie recalled her professional association with Virginia: "She liked my writing and the Hogarth Press published my book about Charlotte of Albany called *Funeral March of a Marionette*. It did not sell very well, but I was always proud and pleased to think that Virginia had liked it."[110]

On August 1, 1938, Virginia writes of the gift of this set of Sand's memoir: "Now you've brought 10 volumes of George Sand on yourself – and a copy I have pasted over the scraps of leather so that it's garish. The original binding was tidy but ugly . But if you disregard this amateurish bookbinding, you'll find – at least I did – that she's a magnificent old woman. Anyhow, do try her when the winter is white and the wolves howling. This Wolf [sic] is so hot after walking on the downs, she can't write. But do some day tell me if you like G.S."

The second letter, unpublished, is about twice the length of the first: Virginia covers both sides of the leaf with four paragraphs, and concludes with an additional pair of lines along the top edge of the first page. The first and third paragraphs, about the Sand, and other books, merit quoting in full:

> It was very nice of you to think of writing to me – I'm so glad you've been enjoying that very shabby copy of George Sand. She's made for reading on long winter evenings – the reason I suppose that none of my busy friends, with all their speechifying & excitements will touch her. I'm so glad you share my enthusiasm .

In the second paragraph Woolf discusses her own life at home:

> I'd give something to see no civilization for miles & I envy you being cut-off. There is an incessant chatter about war, everyday a new rumour, some hysterical editor wants to be soothed by Leonard. But we've escaped London at the moment; only as we're moving – to 37 Mecklenburgh Square – this month, we ran up & down, arranging what's to go where, getting bookcases – you can imagine. But it's nice, overlooking the Foundlings & much greater than 52 T.S. [Tavistock Square] .

83. Virginia Woolf, *Three Guineas*

London: The Hogarth Press, 1938
Private collection

First edition of Virginia's polemic on the prevention of war, with five illustrations by Vanessa; 16,250 copies were printed (Kirkpatrick A23a, Woolmer 440). A presentation copy, inscribed on the front endpaper to Ethel Smyth who "was important in helping Woolf to realize the anger that fuels *Three Guineas*"[111]: *Ethel from Virginia*. With dozens of Ethel's marginal pencil lines and notes throughout – occasionally in disagreement with Virginia – and four measures of music written out in pencil opposite the first text page. Woolf sent this copy to Ethel on June 2, 1938; she wrote on June 1, "I will send you 3 guineas (the book only I mean) tomorrow. I hadn't meant to, as it only repeats *The Years*, with facts to prove it, not fiction; and it is a hurried piece of work – though it was hard work collecting the facts – and you won't like it or agree with it. So let's say no more about it." On June 3, 1938, Smyth replied, "Your book is so splendid that it makes me hot," which Woolf translated into her diary, "A bit of ecstasy from Ethel."[112]

Smyth, whose intellectual brilliance was evinced not only in music but also in politics – through her work for woman suffrage and other feminist activities – captured Virginia's attention in 1909. Virginia reviewed some of Ethel's autobiographical writing in the 'teens and 'twenties (and in the '30s, at Ethel's request, would read new texts in manuscript), and in her 1920 article, "The Intellectual Status of Women," she numbered Ethel among examples of great women who had been victimized by patriarchal oppression. They met, finally, in February 1930, during a visit by Ethel that initiated the friendship that, in Hussey's words, "dominated the last decade of Woolf's life."[113] Virginia detailed that first visit in her diary on February 21, 1930:

> behold a bluff, military old woman (older than I expected), bounced into the room, a little glazed flyaway & abrupt; in a three cornered hat & tailor made suit.
>
> We talked – she talked more than I. (On the stairs going up to tea I had asked to be Virginia; about ten minutes after tea she asked to be Ethel: all was settled; the basis of an undying friendship made in 15 minutes: – how sensible; how rapid;). So sincere & abrupt is she, & discriminating withal – judging Vita & her second rate women friends shrewdly. She says writing music is like writing novels. There is something fine & tried & experienced about her besides the rant & the riot & the egotism – & I'm not sure that she is the egotist that people make out . Has to live in the country because of her passion for games. Plays golf, rides a bicycle; was thrown hunting two years ago . A fine old creature, certainly, Ethel.[114]

After that first meeting, they wrote each other regularly; Virginia received, during the summer of 1930, two letters a day, in response to which "Virginia wrote what amounted to an epistolary autobiography."[115] Ethel has been posited not just as the model for Rose Pargiter in *The Years*, but as a partial model for Mrs. Manresa in *Between the Acts*. Ethel dedicated *As Time Went On*, the 1936 installment of her memoir, to Woolf.

Ethel's ardor, conceived during her initial reading of *A Room of One's Own* and nurtured by that first tea in 1930, went unrequited. On August 25, 1930, Virginia tried to nail down her elusive feelings for her older admirer:

> Lying in my chair in the firelight she looked 18; she looked a young vigorous handsome woman. Suddenly this vanishes; then there is the old crag that has been beaten on by the waves: the humane battered face that makes one respect human nature: or rather feel that it is indomitable & persistent. Then, she is worldly; by which I mean something I like; unembarrassed, aired, sunned, acquainted with this way of life & that; lived in many societies; taken her own way in shirt & tie vigorously unimpeded; ... She has a lightning speed of perception which I liken to my own. But she is more robust; better grounded on fact that I am.

Virginia admired her, praised "her style in writing memoirs," and found her "a game old bird ... what I like is the indomitable old crag; & a certain smile, very wide & benignant. But dear me I am not in love with Ethel. And oh yes – her experience."[116]

IX. The Next Generation
Virginia's Nephews Julian and Quentin Bell

Lettice Ramsey?, *Julian Bell, Virginia Woolf and Quentin Bell*
Charleston, 1931?
Reprinted by permission of the Harvard Theatre Collection, The Houghton Library

"Bubbling and boiling and frizzling": Virginia and the Next Generation   Peter Stansky

The very heart of the Bloomsbury Group was the two Stephen sisters: Virginia and Vanessa. Their brother, Thoby, played a crucial role in introducing his sisters to his Cambridge friends, most notably their husbands, Clive Bell and Leonard Woolf. Their marriages to the sisters, Clive in 1907, Leonard in 1912, were to some extent precipitated by Thoby's tragic early death in 1906. Their younger brother, Adrian, though living with his sisters in Bloomsbury, never appeared to be at the heart of their intellectual and emotional lives. The emotional center came to include Vanessa's children, Julian born in 1908, Quentin in 1910, and Angelica in 1918. To some degree, the husbands felt somewhat excluded from that center and could be a bit envious of the closeness of the sisters and of their deep attachment to the three children. Even Virginia felt at times a little on the outside, and might have regretted the decision that she not have children. As she wrote in her diary on September 13, 1919: "Do I envy Nessa her overflowing household? Perhaps at moments."

Nevertheless, Virginia adored, in her way, all of Vanessa's children. As she wrote to her sister in 1919: "I see my influence will be required not so much to keep my nephews straight as to crookify them." Julian and Quentin were immensely fond of Virginia, as well, but enjoyed finding her at times something of a comic character, prone to act in odd and unpredictable ways. She entered into their world, cooperating with them in producing the household newspaper, *The Charleston Bulletin*. It was at Charleston, the home Vanessa shared with Duncan Grant in Sussex, near to the Woolfs at Monk's House in Rodmell, that the families had their happiest times, as captured in the *Bulletin* and in family photographs. Virginia included them all in *Orlando* (1928): Angelica appears in a photograph as a Russian princess. In the Preface among the list of the great and the good she mentions the "singularly penetrating, if severe, criticism of my nephew Mr. Julian Bell," and thanks Quentin, "an old and valued collaborator in fiction."

Quentin's interests, however, were in the visual arts; he did not seek advice and was in no sense a rival. It was not until after her death that he revealed his great skills as a writer, most notably in his 1972 biography of her that did so much to build interest in both Virginia and Bloomsbury. In his youth, she delighted in writing stories for the *Bulletin* that Quentin illustrated, and in sending him relaxed letters emphasizing the comic and the absurd. Angelica too did not wish to pursue a literary career. Virginia was very pleased at how they all were developing, as she wrote to Vanessa in 1929: "It is very exciting – the extreme potency of your Brats; they might have been nincompoops, instead of bubbling and boiling and frizzling like so many pans of sausages on the fire."

Yet, of the three, her relationship with Julian was the most complex, and it had its ups and downs. There was the ghost of Thoby – christened Julian Thoby Stephen – for whom Julian was named. As she noted on August 2, 1924, in her diary: "Julian has just been & gone, a tall young man, who inveterately believing myself to be young as I do, seems to me like a younger brother. His school continues Thoby's school." And she remarked of him in 1928: "Julian is a vast fat powerful sweet tempered engaging young man, into whose arms I let myself fall, half sister, half mother, & half (but arithmetic denies this) the mocking stirring contemporary friend."

Julian wanted to be a writer, and this presented problems. As with friends, perhaps even more so with relatives, how does one work out ways of being supportive, but also of giving helpful criticism that might in fact be wounding? Virginia was quite self-aware that she could be jealous of other writers, and Julian was not exempt from this – "The usual generation jealousy," she called it in her memoir of Julian. Almost with relief when his first book of poems came out she remarked, "He is no poet." And yet, throughout his earliest literary and intellectual trials and failures, she made significant efforts to be helpful. Not surprisingly Julian was quite sensitive in calibrating the character of her criticism. He was having difficulty in finding his way. He made two attempts at a Fellowship at King's College, Cambridge, where he had been an undergraduate, one with an essay on Alexander Pope and one on Philosophy, in which he had no training, and failed in both. He did secure a position as a Professor of English at Wuhan University in China, cut short when his affair with the wife of the Dean was discovered by her husband. While he was there Virginia wrote him wonderful chronicle letters in which she discusses her reading and writing, and comments on his. Woolf continually exhorts her nephew to write.

In 1936 Virginia convinced Leonard to publish Julian's second book of poetry, *Work for the Winter*, but by then he felt no longer that he was primarily a poet.

Virginia was nevertheless increasingly concerned about Julian and his inability to discover what he would do with his life. He complained that Bloomsbury had taught him no "job." Upon his return from China, Julian was eager to be active in politics and to prepare himself with military experience for the war that was coming. He wished to do that by fighting for the Republic in the Spanish Civil War, much to his mother's and aunt's distress. As a compromise he went as an ambulance driver. And then on July 18, 1937, he was killed. It was an absolutely devastating blow to the sisters, more so of course to his mother. As Virginia remarked in her diary: "Julian had some queer power over her: the lover as well as the son."

So too the love for Vanessa that Virginia and Julian shared was a bond between them. "Our love of Nessa was I think the deepest union between us."[117] Virginia devoted herself to her sister's care in the weeks after his death. And at the end of July she wrote a memoir of Julian, just for herself. At this point, she somewhat rejected the comparison with Thoby, that he was too much of a Bell, "much rougher, more impulsive; more vigorous than Thoby." She found him both at times childish but also serious, and felt that he had really grown up when he came back from China.

The deaths of her brother Thoby and her nephew Julian, 31 years apart, in some sense frame the history of the Bloomsbury Group. In 1906, two years after the Stephen children had moved from Kensington to Bloomsbury, the accomplishments of the Group were in the future. By the time of Julian's death in 1937, the members of the Group were in many cases established figures of great accomplishments, but that also meant that they had detractors. Julian, though so close to his mother and proud of his heritage, was eager to make his own mark, to be his own person. Quentin was more relaxed in going his own way, as an artist and as a writer, yet within the traditions of his family. Virginia adored them both, as well as Angelica, yet bitterly lamented the waste of Julian's death, and its destruction of Vanessa's happiness. It was better, as she said, than dying in Flanders, but so much better not to have died at all, and to have continued as a beloved nephew. As with Thoby, as with Julian, her intense love as well as her devastating loss is deeply evident.

Lettice Ramsey?, *Julian Bell*

Lettice Ramsey?, *Quentin Bell*

84. *Angelica Bell*

For *Orlando*. Ca. late-1920s

Reprinted by permission of the Harvard Theatre Collection, The Houghton Library

Angelica's frustrated claim that she had been given no "center" could have been prefigured by the crisis of her naming. "First called Susannah, then registered as Helen Vanessa; then her mother added Angelica when she was three months old."[118] Not formally educated, she was drawn more to drama than to the other arts – though as an adolescent some of her pottery designs were produced and late in life she published a memoir. She appears in *Orlando* not just, with her brothers, in Virginia's grateful preface, but in a photo as the princess Sasha. In 1942 she married Bunny Garnett – 26 years her senior, her father's former lover and an admirer whose love went unrequited by her mother. They separated in the late 1960s, having had four daughters.

85. Lettice Ramsey, *Julian Bell*

1931

Private collection

A photo of Julian by his lover, Lettice Ramsey, a professional photographer.

Virginia's nephew Julian was born in 1908 and named for her brother (Julian) Thoby Stephen, who had died two years earlier at the age of 26. He grew up among the Bloomsbury Group and published, before his death, two books of poetry – *Winter Movement* (1930) and *Work for the Winter* (1936) – and a book of essays he edited: *We Did Not Fight* (1935). He was also included in the 1932 Hogarth Press anthology *New Signatures*, along with Lehmann, Auden, Day-Lewis, and Spender, among others. Virginia offered Julian emotional and intellectual tutelage throughout his short life. Her letters to him are filled with reactions to his writing, discussion of her own prose and reading, and family news. They are also replete with local gossip, which for Woolf consisted primarily of reports of the literary, artistic, and personal developments within Bloomsbury.

Julian was fatally wounded in July 1937 while driving an ambulance for loyalists in the Spanish Civil War, a concussive blow to the Stephen sisters and their circle. Virginia spent several weeks after his death caring for her sister. Later that year, while struggling with the final draft of *Three Guineas*, she wrote to Vanessa: "Somehow he stirred me up to argue – I wish I'd got his essays to read – they might give me some ideas." In 1938 she compiled for the Press *Julian Bell: Essays, Poems, and Letters*, to which she contributed this memoir of Julian be-

cause she feared not that "time destroyed people," but that "it brushes away the actual personal present." Her recollections include the most intimate moments she spent with him, just before he left for China to teach English in 1935. She realized then "that he never doubted the warmth of my feelings: that I had very strong affections." She also wrote of their final meeting, the night before he left for Spain. They range from his physical appearance ("very fine to look at," though he was "amazingly careless of dress, always"), to his intellectual development, to a comparison between him and Thoby ("Thoby had a natural style, and Julian had not"), to her regrets: "This is the one thing I regret in our relationship: that I might have encouraged him more as a writer . Seeing how immensely generous he was to me about what I did – touchingly proud sometimes of my writings."

86. W. H. Hudson, *The Purple Land*

Being the narrative of one Richard Lamb's adventures in the Banda Oriental, in South America, as told by himself

> London: Duckworth, 1919
> Private collection

First edition, fifth printing. A gift inscribed by Virginia on the front endpaper in pencil: *Julian Bell from Uncle Leonard & Aunt Virginia.* The inscription is undated, but whether presented just after publication, when Julian was eleven years old, or in later years, Virginia likely found this adventure tale an appropriate gift for her nephew, engaged in his own literary experiments and planning his world travels even in his youth. Almost certainly unaware that Hudson had criticized *The Voyage Out* in a 1915 letter to Edward Garnett, Virginia had admired his work from an early age. In critiquing Julian's poetry in 1927, she cited his success: " I understand that you are not trying to write about moods so much as about your feelings as a naturalist. But I think both [Richard] Jefferies and Hudson succeed because they are very careful what they observe; I mean, they do not make a catalogue of things, but choose this that and the other."

Though she called upon Hudson the naturalist to inspire Julian, Virginia herself drew much from his literary essays. In 1916 she published a *TLS* review of his collection of essays on obscure writers, *A Quiet Corner in a Library.* In her description of his approach, we see a clear model for her own essay composed almost a decade later, "The Lives of the Obscure." She writes that Hudson "frankly acknowledges the obscurity of his heroes, and, by demonstrating that their writing was often extremely dull, persuades us to find a good deal of amusement in it. But, having all the facts at his fingers' ends, he can do what is more to the point – he can show us why it is that men like Carey and Lillo, while themselves unimportant, are yet interesting figures in the history of literature."

Two years later she was full of praise for *Far Away and Long Ago*, finding in it "literary and artistic merit" and full of humanity:

> One does not want to recommend it as a book so much as to greet it as a person, and not the clipped and imperfect person of ordinary autobiography, but the whole and complete person whom we meet rarely enough in life or in literature… to read his book is to read another chapter in that enormous book which is written from time to time by Rousseau and Borrow and George

Sand and Aksakoff among other people – a book which we can never read enough of; and therefore we must beg Mr. Hudson not to stop here, but to carry the story on to the farthest possible limits.

In a 1922 letter written several months after his death, she was more equivocal: "Parts of his books are very good – only others are very bad; isn't that so?"

87. H. G. Wells, *The First Men in the Moon*
London: Macmillan and Co., 1920
Private collection

A later, inexpensive edition that circulated amongst five members of the Bloomsbury circle. Another gift from Virginia and Leonard to Julian, inscribed on the front endpaper: *Julian from Uncle Leonard & Aunt Virginia.* Julian initialed the book beneath this inscription. Later from the library of Maynard Keynes; a pencil note on the front pastedown in the hand of Stephen Keynes reads, "Given to Julian Bell by Leonard & Virginia Woolf and later in the possession of Maynard Keynes." Roger Senhouse, a late intimate of Keynes, initialed this page as well, and another small pencil note on the front endpaper – "SK ex JMK" – confirms the transfer to Stephen.

Leonard was a sometime friend and political colleague of Wells, with whom he worked on the establishment of the League of Nations, and whose talks and essays he and Virginia published: *Democracy Under Revision* (1927), *The Common Sense of World Peace* (1929), *The Open Conspiracy* (1930), and *The Idea of a World Encyclopedia* (1936). In his memoirs, however, he confessed to times of *sturm und drang* in the relationship, which had to have been exacerbated by his wife's fundamental dislike of Wells and his work. That Virginia bestowed on Julian one of Wells's best-known scientific romances – purchased, according to a discrete bookplate, from a book shop in Richmond – we attribute to a combination of the early vintage of the presentation, and her sensitivity to the literary predilections of a teenage boy.

Virginia repeatedly castigated Wells in essays and reviews, for his Edwardian aesthetics and his views on women. On Christmas Day 1922 she wrote to Gerald Brenan that it was better to "catch a glimpse" of the human soul, as she and her contemporaries were striving to do, "than to sit down with Hugh Walpole, Wells, etc. etc. and make large oil paintings of fabulous fleshy monsters complete from top to toe." In a 1923 diary entry she considered her growing reputation, and wrote, not without resentment, "I am never praised except by my contemporaries or youngers. When Wells picks young writers, he neglects me."[119] A few years later she describes a visit to Wells and his wife: "Wells remarkable only for a combination of stockishness with acuity: he has a sharp nose, & the cheeks & jowl of a butcher . I could see from the plaintive watery look on Mrs. Wells' face that he is arrogant lustful & bullying in private life. The virtues he likes are courage & vitality." After a second visit she writes of him as "an odd mixture of bubble and solidity. In all this he showed himself, as Desmond said afterwards, perfectly content to be himself, aware of his powers, – aware that he need not take any trouble, since his powers were big enough."[120] These powers, she sensed, could be useful to her. In 1927 when he submitted *Democracy Under Revision* Virginia recorded, though perhaps not without a hint of sarcasm, "This is a great rise in the world for us."[121]

But it was Wells's comments on women and their place in society that truly incensed Woolf, enough to spur her on in *Three Guineas* (1938): "how she must be ancillary & decorative in the world of the future, because she has been tried, in 10 years, & has not proved anything."[122] After that she was always at odds with his work. In 1934 she perused his autobiography, "with interest & distaste."[123] And in 1937, still nearly a decade before his death, she wrote of another visit: "Wells rather shrunk. Lines more marked. He was very affable ," until the subject of T. S. Eliot arose, "& then proceeded to say how he, which I think meant we, had been the death of English literature." She concludes, "A humane man in some corner; also brutal; also entirely without poetry."[124]

88. Clark B. Firestone, *The Coasts of Illusion*

A study of travel tales
With drawings by Ruth Hambidge

New York and London: Harper & Brothers Publishers, 1924
Private collection

Inscribed by Woolf on the front endpaper in her violet ink: *Julian Bell from Leonard & Virginia / 4th Feb 1925.* (Someone has vigorously crossed out the date in blue ink.) With the ownership signature of Peter John Higgens, a relation of a family servant, to whom the book devolved.

An excellent gift for anyone's young nephew, this volume "gives a view of the earth and its inhabitants as seen through the haze of distance, whether of space or of time . It treats of various countries and races and animals which are, or were, or might have been. Although their true domain is the imagination, their supposed domain is, or was, somewhere on the earth" (preface). Accompanied by woodcuts for chapters such as "Denizens of the Deep," "The Pygmies," "Islands of Enchantment," and "The Dream Quests of Spain" – where Julian would meet his untimely death. Such stuff would have sparked the imagination of one such as Julian, who would travel widely and cross-culturally in his too short life.

89. Virginia Woolf, *Autograph and typed letters signed to Julian Bell*

1927–1936
Private collection

Twenty-four letters and 16 postcards, to Julian Bell: 7 TLS, "Virginia" or "V."; 8 TL with Virginia's name typed; 8 ALS; 1 AL; 15 APS; 1 TP. The letters, written almost exclusively from 52 Tavistock Square, London, and Monk's House, Rodmell, span from ca. March 1927 through November 14, 1936; their length varies from a single page to a six-page "diary" letter, the style Virginia adopted while Julian was abroad teaching English in China.

In these affectionate letters Woolf counsels Julian on his writing, discussion of her own prose and reading, and family news; her missives are replete with local gossip, which for Woolf consisted primarily of news of the literary, artistic, and personal worlds of the Bloomsbury circle. The short list of writers Woolf comments on or refers to includes her husband and co-founder of the Hogarth Press

Leonard Woolf; Lord Byron; Stephen Spender; Roger Fry, about whom Woolf was writing a biography; A. E. Housman; E. M. Forster; Edith Sitwell; Vita Sackville-West; John Dryden; Lytton Strachey; Wyndham Lewis; Christopher Isherwood; Aldous Huxley; Shakespeare; and T. S. Eliot.

The most significant of the characters frequently appearing in Woolf's letters is Eliot. Woolf records her own reaction to the poet and his work, and vividly recounts audience response at the first staging of *Murder in the Cathedral*:

> ... I had almost to carry Leonard out, shrieking. What was odd was how much better it reads than acts; the tightness, chillness, deadness and general worship of the decay and skeleton made one near sickness. The truth is when he has live bodies on the stage his words thin out, and no rhetoric will save them. There we met Stephen Spender, who also was green at the gills with dislike.

In May of 1930 Woolf had offered a thumbnail critique of *Ash Wednesday*, writing, "Tom's hard boiled egg is hard boiled ... all this damnable Mary and Mother and God. Still he can write"; and over five years later: "... [Eliot's] determined to write plays about modern life in verse. And rather crusty when reviewers say he's an old fogy. In fact I think he feels that he's only just beginning to write what he wants. Whether he's on the turn, religiously speaking, I'm not sure...."

In May of 1936, not long before Julian's death, Woolf mused about the state of literary affairs:

> Old Blooms[bur]y may have more blood in it than you think. I get the most astonishing elaborate letters from poet Eliot; who is now the titular head of English-American letters since the death yesterday of [A. E.] Housman.... Do you like his muse? I don't altogether; why, I can't say. Always too laden with a peculiar scent for my taste. May, death, lads, Shropshire. But they say he was a great scholar, and I can remember when his Manilius came out.... Where he fails is when he takes on him to be a burly Englishman, with our gift for character drawing. Not a touch of Dickens or Shakespeare are in him. Last night I read Midsummer Night's Dream. Well there you have it — all England all may in a song or two....

Virginia captures the spirit of the period in which she lived and wrote through personal anecdote, and illustrates the practice of literary Modernism – as she had help to develop it – through her critique of Julian's own emerging style. Woolf continually exhorts her nephew to write – poetry, prose, anything but a novel – and gorges herself on his occasional success. Still, she "thought him careless, not an 'artist,'" and told him in one letter, encapsulating beautifully the developing Modernist ideal: "... But of course you will have to learn to express yourself more fluently. I do not mean by that only that you will have to get greater command of words and use more of them. I think you will have to learn to leave out details, even though they are good in themselves, so as to give a more generalised view...," adding, "I will always give you good advice...." He seems to have taken her criticism well. They continued to correspond, and just over a year to the day later, Virginia reiterates her suggestions: "I think the first nature poems still suffer to some extent from your old disease of crowded detail, so thick one can't see the whole."

In her memoir of Julian she published in 1938, Virginia expresses regret having lightheartedly rejected a piece he sent her on Roger Fry, which cooled him slightly, temporarily, towards her. But she also admits to his power to hurt her, with "his rather caustic teasing, something like Clive's, and I felt it more because I have suffered from Clive's caustic and rather cruel teasing in the past. – Julian had something of the same way of 'seeing through one'; but it was less personal, and stronger." Nevertheless, "our relationship was perfectly secure because it was founded on our passion – not too strong a word for either of us – for Nessa."

90. Julian Bell, *Work For The Winter, More Or Less For Christmas*

Privately printed, 1935
Private collection

Simply bound paper pamphlet with black lettering on front. A presentation copy, inscribed to G.W.H. Rylands: *To Dadie (who is to a certain extent responsible) from Julian.*

Winter Movement And Other Poems

London: Chatto and Windus, 1930
Private collection

First edition

Work For The Winter And Other Poems

Hogarth Living Poets, Second Series, No. 4
London: The Hogarth Press, 1936
Private collection

First edition; 750 copies printed.

91. Virginia Woolf?, *Julian Bell, Angelica Bell, Lettice Ramsey*

Ca. 1931
Reprinted by permission of the Harvard Theatre Collection, The Houghton Library

92. Lettice Ramsey?, *Julian Bell*

1931
Reprinted by permission of the Harvard Theatre Collection, The Houghton Library

93. Lettice Ramsey?, *Quentin Bell*

1931
Reprinted by permission of the Harvard Theatre Collection, The Houghton Library

94. Virginia Woolf, *Typed letters signed to Quentin*

August 30–December 21, 1933
Private collection

A series of four letters, typed and signed by Virginia, with her occasional manuscript corrections to characteristic typographical errors, as well as occasional insertions and revisions to her text. Virginia writes of her activities, a recent plagiarism from *A Room of One's Own* in the *New Statesman* by a school girl, Christmas shopping, her moves from country to city, and back, and the life and work of her many visitors. She describes them physically, and inserts lines of dialogue – with friends such as Vita (who is tapped for her knowledge of plant life), Ottoline (who sends her memoirs: "of course she lies, but not entirely . Since Helene of Troy I don't think any woman can have launched so many ships"), Ethel Smyth (who hounds her), Mary Hutchinson (who visits), Sickert ("was so much impressed that Nessa made me write to him … do you think one could treat his paintings like novels?"), Stephen Spender ("talks incessantly and will pan out in years to come a prodigious bore. But he's a nice poetic youth; big nosed, bright eyed, like a giant thrush"), as well as with neighbors and acquaintances like Neil Lyons ("He is claret colored and barrel bodied"), Michael Arlen ("a rubber faced little sweaty Armenian monkey"), Princess Bibesco, and Wogan Philipps, then still Rosamond Lehmann's husband ("only a scampering terrier brained painter," November 18). She is, as usual, prone to hyperbolic exclamations:

> So it went from lunacy to lunacy, till the moon rose and the dogs bayed. Oh my dear Quentin, that I were a seal lying on a slab of ice in the Hebrides, save that if I were Ethel Smyth would bawl me Brahms in such tones, so she says, that the male seal gives cover copulating, and dives into the deep. So Orpheus you remember charmed the trees (August 30).

Irreverent as always, she addresses the unconventional lifestyles of many of their friends. She proposes calling Spender, Plomer, Auden, and their partners the "Lilies of the Valley." "Their great sorrow at the moment is Siegfried Sassoon's defection; he's gone and married a woman, and says that he has never till now known what love meant. It is the saving of life he says; and this greatly worries the Lilies of the Valley among whom is Morgan of course, who loves a crippled bootmaker; why this passion for the porter, the policeman and the bootmaker? Well, we must go into the matter when you come back" (December 21).

She includes much gossip of Ralph Partridge, then dividing his time between Ham Spray House (where he had lived with Lytton Strachey and Carrington, before their recent deaths), and with Frances:

> Wogan told us such stories of the Partridges, and how poor Fanny rang him twice in one day to drive 30 miles to Ham Spray. 'Ralph's killing himself. Come at once.' So off he went, and then old Ralph emerged like a great baboon from some bushes. But is over now – Ralph appears stark naked with a cup of tea in his hand by your bed at eight in the morning. I think Lytton's ghost would give a little shiver. It's Lytton played by bumpkins – Lytton acted in the kitchen (November 18).

She also tells of Victor bringing Barbara a box full of rubies. "Well, I won't be indiscreet, but between you and me, that's a marriage bound for the rocks. Victor would make me shoot him in ten minutes. He's a Jew; that I rather like but, – no, I won't be indiscreet" (November 26). This letter she closes with remarks on Ottoline's memoirs: "I wish I could lend them to you, to reveal old Bloomsbury at its height; but I dare not. Human nature is in odd mixture – isn't it – now take Roger. But I leave you to follow up the reflection as I must go and make tea."

X. The Group at and after Her Death

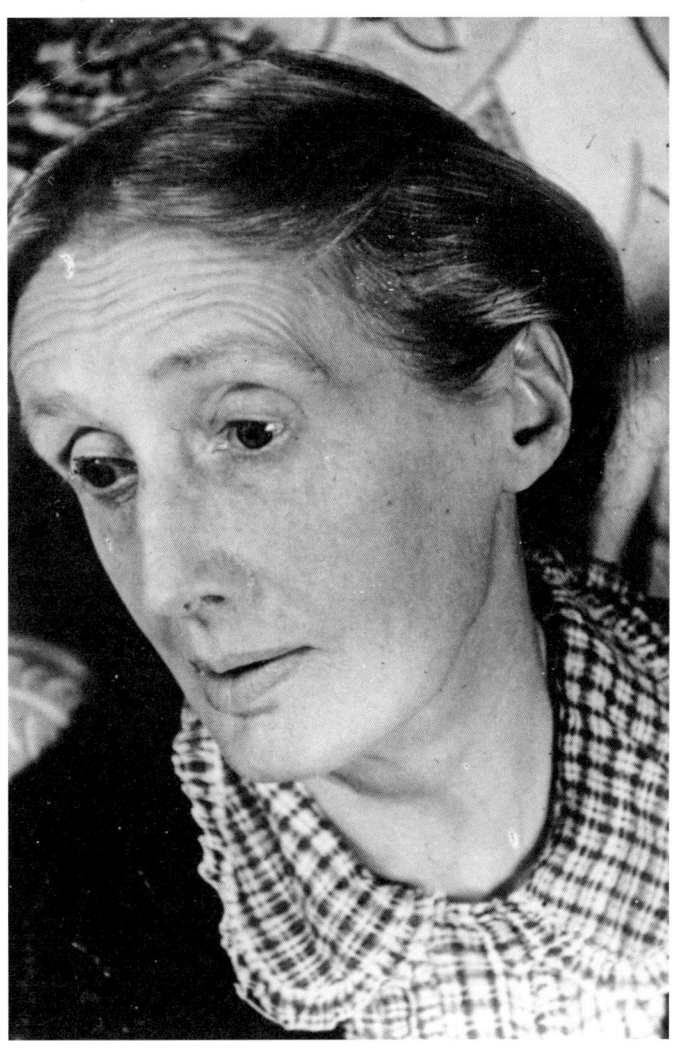

Gisèle Freund, *Virginia Woolf*
1939
Private collection

Ontology of a Suicide Andrew Solomon

There are two inaccurate common views of Virginia Woolf. The first is that her depressions were episodic and that she was in her better moods free of melancholy, and the other is that she lived her life in darkness, with only partial and infrequent remissions from severe depression. The fact of her charm can blind us to her persistent agony, and the fact of her suicide can blind us to her enduring ecstasy. Both her work and her life demonstrate an extraordinary entwining of these qualities; for Woolf, all experience is permanently suffused with relentless vitality and blunt tragedy. While what clinicians would describe as depression may have been intermittent in her life, a sense of everything's sadness hums through even her work's brightest evocations. Sadness need not obscure beauty; indeed it often enhances it. Nor does it contravene the ineffable bliss inherent in the very fact of awareness, a bliss as strong in the awareness of sorrow as in the awareness of joy.

This potent dualism is evoked with particular intensity in her underrated early novel *Jacob's Room*. In the very landscape she notes it: "No doubt if this were Italy, Greece, or even the shores of Spain, sadness would be routed by strangeness and excitement and the nudge of a classical education. But the Cornish hills have stark chimneys standing on them; and, somehow or other, loveliness is infernally sad. Yes, the chimneys and the coastguard stations and the little bays with waves breaking unseen by anyone make one remember the overpowering sorrow. And what can this sorrow be? It is brewed by the earth itself. It comes from the houses on the coast. We start transparent, and then the cloud thickens. All history backs our pane of glass. To escape is vain." The ubiquity of this sadness is likewise summoned in every genre scene, where it seems almost ludicrous: "Yet she had the rapt look of one brushing through crowds on a summer's afternoon and the tumult of the present seems like an elegy for past youth and past summers, and there rose in her mind a curious sadness, as if time and eternity showed through skirts and waistcoats and she saw people passing tragically to destruction. Yet, heaven knows, Julia was no fool; a sharper woman at a bargain did not exist, and she was always punctual." Finally and explicitly, it surfaces in the heart even of the most engaged and well-adjusted of men, Jacob in this case simply looking out the window at strangers walking in the street below: "Their lack of concern for him was not the cause of his gloom, but some more profound conviction – it was not that he himself was lonely, but that all people are." This desolation, inherent in the human condition, seems strange when it reaches consciousness, irrelevant to the concrete experiences it constantly shadows, inconsistent with the practical reality of our capacity to function. It is our folly to think of bargains when the world is full of such deep stuff – or perhaps it is our redemption, the very thing that allows us to continue in the fabric of our lives.

Five years after *Jacob's Room,* Woolf published *To the Lighthouse,* and in it describes over and over again the impossibility of reconciling these extremes of sentiment. She acknowledges not only the sadness, but also how that sadness may be forever within view of happiness. "Always, Mrs Ramsay felt, one helped oneself out of solitude reluctantly by laying hold of some little odd and end, some sound, some sight. She listened, but it was all very still; cricket was over; the children were in their baths; there was only the sound of the sea. She stopped knitting; she held the long reddish-brown stocking dangling in her hands for a moment. She saw the light again. With some irony in her interrogation, for when one woke at all, one's relations changed, she looked at the steady light, the pitiless, the remorseless, which was so much her, yet so little her, which had her at its beck and call (she woke in the night and saw it bent across their bed, stroking the floor), but for all that she thought, watching it with fascination, hypnotized, as if it were stroking with its silver fingers some sealed vessel in her brain whose bursting would flood her with delight, she had known happiness, exquisite happiness, intense happiness, and it silvered the rough waves a little more brightly, as daylight faded, and the blue went out of the sea and it rolled in waves of pure lemon which curved and swelled and broke upon the beach and the ecstasy burst in her eyes and waves of pure delight raced over the floor of her mind and she felt, It is enough! It is enough!"

It is in the moment of feeling sorrowful that such optimism suddenly dawns, as dramatic an opposite as when Jacob's sadness manifests in the thick of contentment. Ultimately, the Ramseys will leave the Hebrides; Mrs. Ramsay will die; and as every sad moment has had this tinge of glory, so each happy one will be compromised by dismay. "Also, the sea tosses itself and breaks itself, and should any sleeper fancying that he might find on the beach an answer to his doubts, a sharer of his solitude, throw off his bedclothes and go down by himself to walk on the sand, no image with semblance of serving and divine promptitude comes readily to hand, bringing the night to order and making the world reflect the compass of the soul." This longing for resolution, which drives human enterprise, is a course of irresolvable frustration. We quest with exquisite desire after a vision that will mitigate our aloneness. Here is Lily Briscoe: "And what was even more exciting, she felt, too, as she saw Mr. Ramsay bearing down and retreating, and Mrs. Ramsay sitting with James in the window and the cloud moving and the tree bending, how life, from being made up of little separate incidents which one lived one by one, became curled and whole like a wave which bore one up with it and threw one down with it, there, with a dash on the beach." Such resolution is always proximate and always elusive, and though it seems like a lasting truth, it is transient. "It seemed now as if, touched by human penitence and all its toil, divine goodness had parted the curtain and displayed behind it, single, distinct, the hare erect; the wave falling; the boat rocking; which, did we deserve them, should be ours always. But alas, divine goodness so confuses them that it seems impossible that their calm should ever return or that we should ever compose from their fragments a perfect whole or read in the littered pieces a clear word of truth."

Woolf narrates life throughout her work in a vocabulary of yearning, always gazing at truth and never able to touch it.

In *Orlando*, published the next year, Woolf is at her most exuberant, and love grants her a view behind that parted curtain. "It cannot be denied that the most successful practitioners of the art of life, often unknown people by the way, somehow contrive to synchronise the sixty or seventy different times which beat simultaneously in every normal human system, so that when eleven strikes, all the rest chime in unison, and the present is neither a violent disruption nor completely forgotten in the past. Of them we can justly say that they live precisely the sixty-eight or seventy-two years allotted them on the tombstone. Of the rest, some we know to be dead, though they walk among us; some are not yet born though they go through the forms of life; others are hundreds of years old though they call themselves thirty-six." This attempt to be within and of the moment, to live in the present and the past with a nod to the future, is the great quest, but it eludes almost everyone. Orlando is finally capable of this purity – but then this is a fairy tale. Woolf describes a moment of true peace. "The whole of her darkened and settled, as when some foil whose addition makes the round and solidity of a surface is added to it, and the shallow becomes deep and the near distant; and all is contained as water is contained by the sides of a well. So she was now darkened, stilled, and became what is called, rightly or wrongly, a real self. And she fell silent. For it is probable that when people talk aloud, the selves (of which there may be more than two thousand) are conscious of disseverment, and are trying to communicate; but when communication is established, there is nothing more to be said." Woolf would not have been immune to the irony that in the work of a writer whose very fabric of existence is words, silence is represented as the ultimate achievement, and that that silence is itself evoked and narrated in words. The state desired is evinced in its opposite.

Orlando may have arrived at the genius of silence, but for Woolf, there is always more to be said, precisely because such harmony remains obscure. Near the end of her life, she wrote in *The Years*, "Take notes and the pain goes away." It is as though Woolf imagined her entire oeuvre as a release from the slavery of her own sorrow, as though the language that flows when there is no true communication among the two thousand selves were both a symptom of and a balm for despair. In her suicide note to Leonard, she said, "I am wasting your life. It is this madness. Nothing anyone says can persuade me. You can work, and you will be much better off without me. You see I can't write this even, which shows I am right." The failure of language for her was the inability to make the pain go away, the failure to find in her own wordlessness a noble silence like Orlando's. People are always interested in the documents that are left behind by someone who commits suicide. While such documents are usually descriptive, in Woolf's case they (the books, the suicide note, all of it) are emblematic. She does not so much use language to make a statement about her decision to end her own life as demonstrate through language why her self-abnegation had become inevitable. Like Lear, Woolf has words as the mechanism of her demise. "These changes of mood wear us out," she wrote in *Jacob's Room*.

In *Between the Acts*, her final book, published posthumously, she wrote, "Thoughts without words, he mused. Can that be?" It's as though her own strategy of note-taking is being called into dramatic question. The irreconcilable permanent contrasts about which she had written so often were becoming intolerable. "Love and hate – how they tore her asunder! Surely it was time that someone invented a new plot, or that the author came out from the bushes...." This could as easily have read that joy and despair were tearing her asunder, that this duality had become unbearably oppressive. Reality is alien to the human intelligence that longs for purity, for reconciliation, for a single powerful truth: for the hare erect; the wave falling; the boat rocking. Woolf describes the author of the play: "She wanted to expose them, as it were, to douche them, with the present-time reality. But something was going wrong with the experiment. 'Reality too strong,' she muttered. And then the rain fell, sudden and profuse. No one had seen the cloud coming. There it was, black, swollen, on top of them. Down it poured like all the people in the world weeping. Tears. Tears. Tears. They trickled down her cheeks as if they were her own tears. But they were all people's tears weeping for all people. The window was all sky without colour. The house had lost its shelter. It was night before roads were made, or houses. It was the night that dwellers in caves had watched from some high place among the rocks. Then the curtain rose. They spoke."

As if a curtain had lifted and the artifice had returned, as if reality had been shunted away for the moment, Woolf tried to save herself through art, and her writing sang in the hope of relinquished pain. The more pain she fled, the more beautiful the celebratory prose became, until she wrote that suicide note which does not merit its own apology. Her choice of water as the medium for her death is striking given all it had meant throughout her work, and this strong final equation of rain and tears. *Between the Acts* is no sadder than her other books. If suicide is the option chosen by those who believe the pain of life outweighs its pleasure, then Woolf's suicide was one born of acute shifting between the states. She had, in the end, a clinical condition that was intolerable and debasing, but the insight drawn from that condition imbues her work and is directly implicated in the radiance she could achieve when the curtain rose. Perhaps the clearest evidence of this mix of pleasure and suffering is belied by Leonard Woolf's writing to Vita, in a letter included in this exhibition, "I don't know whether it is a strange thing, but I keep on thinking how amused Virginia would have been by the extraordinary things people write to me about her." This idea of a Virginia Woolf who would have laughed even in the wake of her own suicide conjures someone for whom the persistence of binary opposites was itself the source of delight and despondency.

95. Virginia Woolf, *Manuscript Diary*

March 24, 1941

The Henry W. and Albert A. Berg Collection of English and American
Literature, Astor Lenox and Tilden Foundations, The New York Public Library

Virginia's manuscript diary, kept in a spiral notebook partially covered in orange cloth, likely by Virginia herself. Labeled by hand, "V.W. Diary 1941," with her characteristic hand-drawn blue vertical line down every page, creating a broad left-hand margin for dates and edits. She used eleven pages in this volume, for ten entries, the final entry dated March 24, 1941.

The characteristic topic and tone of this entry belies the turmoil that had begun again a few weeks previous. She describes a woman they have visited in her first lengthy paragraph: "And before 5 minutes had passed she had told us that two of her sons had been killed in the war. Sitting there I tried to coin a few compliments. But they perished in the icy sea between us. And then there was nothing." She moves on to discuss, literally, the weather, and muses, "This windy corner. And Nessa is at Brighton, & I am imagining how it wd be if we could infuse souls." After mentioning some correspondence chores on her agenda, she concludes, "L. is doing the rhododendrons." It's true that Virginia had not been well for weeks, but by the 24th Leonard thought he saw improvement. It did not last. Virginia wrote to her sister on March 28,

> I feel that I have gone too far this time to come back again. I am certain now that I am going mad again. It is just as it was the first time, I am always hearing voices, and I know I shant get over it now. I can hardly think clearly any more. If I could I would tell you what you and the children have meant to me. I think you know. I have fought against it, but I cant any longer.

She also writes, as she does in a separate letter to Leonard, of their profound happiness: he has been "astonishingly good," "[i]t was all due to you. No one could have been so good as you have been, from the very first day till now. Everyone knows that."

96. Vanessa Bell and Leonard Woolf, *Autograph letters signed to Vita Sackville-West*

March 28–April 6, 1941

Private collection

A series of letters Vanessa and Leonard wrote to Vita upon Virginia's disappearance and presumed death. Virginia had written to both Leonard and Vanessa on March 28, 1941, with dire predictions, and Leonard writes that same day to Vita:

> I do not want you to see in the paper or hear possibly on the wireless the terrible thing that has happened to Virginia. She has been really very ill these last weeks & was terrified that she was going mad again. It was, I suppose, the strain of the war & finishing her book & she could not rest or eat. Today she went for a walk leaving behind a letter saying that she was committing suicide. I think she has drowned herself as I found her stick floating in the river, but we have not found

the body. I know what you will feel & what you felt for her. She was very fond of you. She has been through hell these last days.

Vanessa writes to Vita on the 29th:

> Leonard said he was with you so this is only because I feel I want to be in touch with you somehow – as the person Virginia loved most I think outside her own family. I was there yesterday by chance & saw him. . . . he was of course amazingly self controlled & calm & insisted on being left alone. There is nothing I can do yet. Perhaps some time you & I could meet? It is difficult I know. But we will manage it presently. Now we can only wait till the first horrors are over which somehow make it almost impossible to feel much .

On April 2 she urges Vita to lunch, and reminiscences about Virginia:

> I remember all those days after I heard about Julian lying in an unreal state & hearing her voice going on & on keeping life going as it seemed when otherwise it would have stopped – and later every day she came to see me here .

She continues, assessing Leonard's state of being:

> He told me if he had it all over again he would do the same — & so I suppose he realizes he's not to blame actually – in fact I think nothing could have prevented the possibility just then – only I wish I had realized it. But I didn't at all. Even the last time when she talked to me about herself that possibility never occurred to me – how strange it seems.

After Vita's visit, she writes, "I liked very much seeing you my dear – I could hardly believe Virginia wasn't there too talking to us " (April 8).

Two weeks later, after Virginia's body was discovered on the bank opposite where Leonard found her walking stick, Vanessa writes to Vita again, explaining her lack of contact at this important time:

> It was another shock of course. & one had so hoped it wouldn't happen. But I think Leonard meant it when he said, as he did to me, that it was no more horrible than all the rest . I think he really felt, as indeed I did too, that all that part of it was very unreal & unimportant. He was the only person called at the inquest & I didn't even know exactly when it was . He arranged for cremation at Brighton yesterday & didn't want me to go so I didn't. There was no ceremony. Nothing. Poor old Ethel [Smyth], who had written to me, apparently wanting a country church yard, will be disappointed, but after all anything else would have been too uncharacteristic.

She then laments Leonard's solitude at Rodmell, but offers hope that he'll have visitors and other distractions.

97. Vita Sackville-West, *In Memoriam: Virginia Woolf*
Corrected typescript, ca. April 1941
Private collection

Leonard Woolf, *Autograph letter signed to Vita Sackville-West*
April 6, 1941
Private collection

Working typescript draft of Vita's tribute to Virginia, with pencil additions, deletions, alterations, and insertions. Composed shortly after Virginia's death in 1941, it appeared in the *Observer* on April 6. Vita transcribed it in type from that appearance – she notes in type at the bottom, "From 'The Observer.' April, 1941" – and continues to revise the text. She opens,

> Many words crowd, and all and each unmeaning.
> The simplest words in sorrow are the best.

She notes how Virginia adapted the pursuits of her childhood into adulthood:

> I remember she told me once that she, a child,
> Trapped evening moths with honey round a tree-trunk,
> And with a lantern watched their antic fight

Here she strikes out "fight" and writes in, "flight."

> So she, a poet, caught her special prey
> With words of honey and lamp of wit.

She goes on to compare Virginia to a moth, however her truest lines reflect her sheer humanity:

> So let us say, she loved the water-meadows,
> The Downs; her books; her friends; her memories;

Here Vita switches the order, circling "her friends" and moving them ahead of her books.

> The room which was her own.
> London by twilight; shows and unknown people

Further editing, Vita changes "unknown people" to "Mrs. Brown," the Mrs. Brown who was her character in search of, well, character in her essay, "Mr. Bennett and Mrs. Brown."

> Donne's church; the Strand; the buses, and the large
> Swell of humanity that passed her by....

She concludes,

> She now has gone
> Into the prouder world of immortality.

Leonard writes to Vita his reaction to the poem: "your poem which I have read this moment moved me profoundly... thank you for it. It expresses perfectly what was Virginia & what one felt." He then suggests a visit, and sends word of a morbid development: "They have been dragging the river the last week, but are now, I think, abandoning the search."

98. Duncan Grant, "*Virginia Woolf*" Obituary

Manuscript material
1941
Private collection

Duncan Grant, "*Virginia Woolf*"

Horizon: A Review of Literature and Art
III.18 (June 1941), pages 402-406
Private collection

Duncan's manuscript notebook, filled from both sides to the center, primarily with manuscript notes and draft text, with occasional transcriptions and drawings. With a printed copy of *Horizon*, in which his reflections appear. Further memoirs of Virginia – by Vita, T.S. Eliot, Rose Macaulay, and William Plomer – appeared in the May 1941 issue (III.17), pages 313-328.

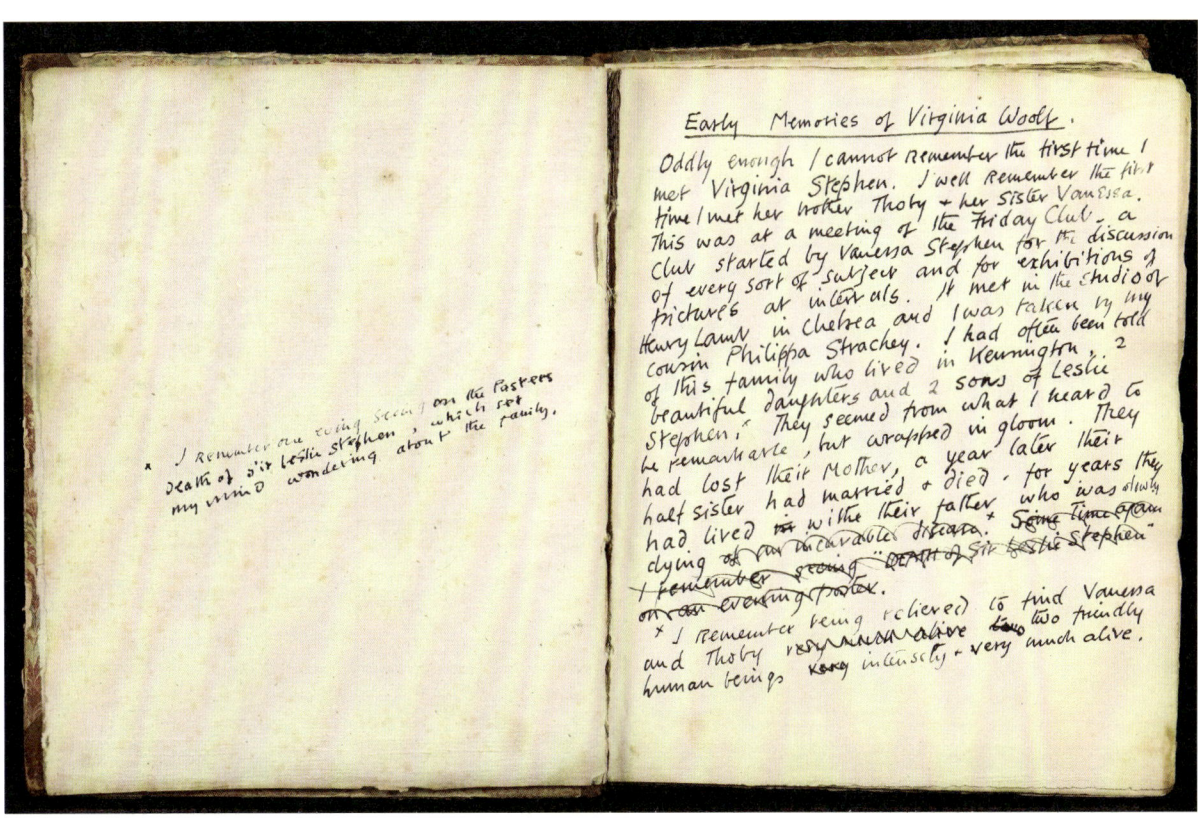

99. Leonard Woolf, *Autograph and typed letters signed to Vita Sackville-West*

May 24–June 23, 1941
Private collection

Leonard wrote to Vita after Virginia's disappearance and death about Virginia's will. His first letter is prompted by the probate lawyers: "Virginia has left you one of her MS with instructions to me to choose it and now the probate people have asked me to inform them which it is to be." He suggests *Flush* or *The Years*. He concludes, "I liked your reminiscences in *Horizon*; they were so characteristic" (May 24). What follows is a series of letters in which Leonard continually haggles with Vita over the issue of which manuscript she will receive. "I am glad you are outspoken, as always, and I will be" (May 29). He wishes to retain *The Waves*, which she had apparently requested. He counters with *Mrs. Dalloway*, and asks if he may have the unpublished portions of *Orlando* in her possession typed. Once he has seen them, he refers to them as "inchoate" and returns them, in this letter, as in the others, discussing Virginia's method of composition (June 2). In the meantime she has apparently suggested *To the Lighthouse*, but for various reasons he feels *Mrs. Dalloway* the better choice (June 14). His final letter (June 23) reads in full:

> Here is the book. I am also sending the MS of *Mrs. Dalloway*. I presume that it is legal for me to do so before the estate is settled. The first vol. is called *The Hours* which is what V. intended the title to be originally.
>
> The garden here has been rather knocked about by the weather. I think I have less fruit than any year since we came here.

Virginia Woolf: Her Courage to Write as a Woman Ruth Gruber

Virginia Woolf did not know when I met her 73 years ago that she would chart the course of my life. Through her writings she taught me to have the courage to write as a woman, think as a woman, cherish integrity, and fight injustice.

I first heard of her in 1931 when I was a 19-year-old American exchange student in the University of Cologne, Germany. The head of the English Department, Professor Herbert Schöffler, called me to his office one morning. He offered me a chair while he hoisted himself up to the edge of his desk. He was a short, stout man with a round jovial face. "We have been watching you. We would like you to stay and get your Ph.D." I was stunned. Getting a Ph.D. in Germany had never entered my mind. "Thank you," I said. "You're very kind but it's impossible. My grant from the Institute of International Education is for only one year."

"It's never been done in one year but maybe you can do it. I have a special motive," he explained. "I would like to have one of my students do original literary research on the writings of Virginia Woolf. She is my favorite modern English author. But my students are Germans; their English is not good enough. I don't know when I shall have another American or English student." He smiled at me paternally. "If you agree, I would like you to write it in English."

My philosophy, even at 19, was dream dreams, have visions, and let no obstacles stop me. "I'll try," I said, "but I must tell you, I never heard of Virginia Woolf, even in the courses I took in modern English literature. She isn't well known in America."

"We know that all too well." He stood up, walked to his bookcase and drew out five of her novels. "These are for you," he said, beaming, "and I suggest you go downtown to get the rest."

I unwrapped them as soon as I returned to the home of the Herz family with whom I was living and soon was mesmerized. I hung her photo on my wall. *A Room of One's Own* became my guide and *Orlando* my favorite novel. I jotted my thoughts in the margins and endpapers of the books and copied sentences I loved, like, "So long as you write what you wish to write, that is all that matters ." I put those sentences on my desk: they were the first things I read when I woke and the last before I went to bed.

That fall, while working on my thesis, I sensed autobiographical strains in *Orlando*, and wrote to Woolf in care of the Hogarth Press to inquire. A few weeks later her secretary, Peggy Belsher, answered my letter. "Mrs. Woolf has always preferred to let her readers decide for themselves as to the meaning of her works, and therefore cannot reply to your questions concerning the autobiographical elements in *Orlando*." However, she continued, the story was based on the life of Vita Sackville-West and the house was Knole, Miss Sackville-West's ancestral home.

In June 1932, I stood for the orals, my knees shaking as I defended my thesis. Two other professors joined in the interrogation. One was Professor Ernst Bertram, the leading Nietzsche scholar in Germany, whose bare unfriendly looking office made the examination like an Inquisition. The other examiner was an art historian. The two professors asked serious questions in their field but they stood fascinated when Professor Shöffler began his questioning on VW. His round face looked grave. "You called her novel *The Waves* a 'rhythm of conflicts.' What did you mean?"

The sentences from my thesis were still fresh in my mind. "It's the struggle between light and darkness. It is the law of polarity, of conflicts as irreconcilable as night and day, of poets versus critics, that reverberate through all her writing." What I did not know in 1932 – or later, in 1935, when I corresponded with her – was that she suffered from manic-depression: she was bi-polar. Leafing through my thesis, I was surprised how often the word "polarity" appeared. I have since learned about the suffering that bi-polar patients endure. One frequent way they deal with their unbearable pain is suicide.

At the end of the orals, which lasted about half an hour, Professor Schöffler told me to wait outside the office. He soon came out, smiling broadly, "Congratulations, you have achieved the doctorate *mit sehr gut* (the German equivalent of magna cum laude). I could hardly breathe. "Thank you, Professor Schöffler, oh thank you." Still smiling, he handed me two critiques, handwritten on a torn piece of paper. My hands shook as I read Professsor Schöffler's first. "It is a critical study of a woman by a woman. A man could never have written this work. It possesses deep critical powers and a profound knowledge of English and world literature." The second was Professor Bertram's critique. Still trembling, I read: "This work could be a model for modern criticism. The struggle of the poet with the critic is seen very sharp, very clearly. The work shows amazing maturity and originality."

The next morning, the Lord Mayor of Cologne, Dr. Konrad Adenauer, invited me to his reception suite in the town hall. Towering over me, he congratulated me and then presented me with two handsome illustrated books on Cologne. "These books, Fräulein Doktor," he said warmly, using my new title, "I hope will help you remember your year among us." I held the books close to my body. "I will never forget this year," I said thinking that I owe all this to Virginia Woolf.

A day later I was astounded to read in the *Frankfürter Zeitung* that a young American woman had done what no young man had done, achieved the doctorate at 20 in one year. But I was in panic when an army of reporters accosted me on the dock in New York as I stepped off the *St. Louis*. One of the reporters shouted at me, "How does it feel to be the youngest Ph.D. in the world?"

I broke through the circle of men, rushed home and soon was accosted by more reporters. A middle-aged man from the *New York Herald Tribune* understood my feelings. His story was titled, "Girl Ph.D., 20, Bewildered By Fuss Over Feat Feels Hunted, Feels Achievement Was Not Unusual." But he did not write one word about Woolf.

In 1935 Tauchnitz, Leipzig, published the thesis as a paperback book. Professor Schöffler had submitted it to them. I found a copy for $1.95 in Barnes & Noble, then a small bookstore and publishing house near NYU. I was preparing to travel abroad on another fellowship to research women under fascism, communism and democracy. With the bravado of youth, I sent Woolf a copy of the published thesis and asked if I could interview her. On May 17th, Margaret West answered on Mrs. Woolf's behalf that the Woolfs were absent in Italy. She would place the book before VW on her return. After months of travel, I reached London and telephoned the Hogarth Press. Miss West was gracious as she extended an invitation from the Woolfs to join them for tea.

I was ecstatic. At 6:00 pm on the appointed day I arrived at 52 Tavistock Square. A uniformed maid greeted me at the street entrance and led me up a dark narrow staircase to the first floor. She knocked on a door and Leonard Woolf answered. He had a long oval face, sad eyes, trembling hands. He greeted me warmly and led me through the large parlor to a winged chair where I sat down only a few inches from Virginia Woolf. She was lying on a rug in front of a blazing fire, dressed in a long, gray gown, gray stockings, gray shoes. Her gray hair was cropped short like a boy's. Two long fingers embraced a silver cigarette holder through which she blew gray smoke. She was elegant, graceful and beautiful. She never smiled. Leonard sat far behind me against the back wall. Yet he seemed to be protectively hovering over her.

I was too overawed to speak. Something was wrong, I told myself, I had come to sit at her feet but she was lying at mine. Virginia broke the silence, with a series of unsettling remarks. "I don't know how I can help you," she puffed on her cigarette. "I don't understand a thing about politics. I never worked a day in my life." It startled me that she did not think publishing ten books, countless essays, and brilliant book reviews, many about politics, was work. She looked vulnerable before the fire. There was another long silence. She smoked dreamily, often gazing into the flames.

This time Leonard broke the silence, "Where have you come from?"

"Siberia and the Soviet Arctic," I murmured.

"The Soviet Arctic?" He pulled his chair next to mine and began grilling me when Virginia interrupted. "We were just in your Germany." (My Germany? I wanted to say that I don't have an ounce of German blood but I would not dare contradict her.) "Our car was stopped to let Hitler and his entourage pass," she continued. "Madness, that country."

"I was in Germany a few months ago," I found the courage finally to say. "I was in a bookstore in Cologne when Hitler's voice came over a loudspeaker. A terrifying voice, as if it came not from his lungs but his bowels."

She agreed, "He has a terrifying voice." She removed the spent cigarette, eased another into the holder and lit it. "There is such horror in the world," she mused, turning her face to the fire.

"That's what strikes me so forcefully in your books," I managed to say. "There's always the hope that women will help end the horror of war and create peace. Men make wars, not women." I thought of *Three Guineas*.

"Once," she nodded, "we had such hope for the world—" Her voice drifted off with her smoke.

I glanced at my watch. It was 6:30. A half hour had passed. I stood up carefully, leaned down, shook her hand, and thanked her. Leonard led me to the door where I shook his hand and departed. I had met Virginia Woolf!

Half a century later, to my surprise, I discovered that most of her letters and diaries were in the Berg Collection at the New York Public Library on Fifth Avenue. I rushed to the library and when I convinced curator Lola Szladits, guardian of the Woolf papers, that I was a serious scholar, she granted access. I felt my heart beating as I held the thin, blue, delicate sheets on which Woolf had written her letters in tiny handwriting. Amazed, almost unbelieving. I discovered references to me in her letters and diaries – references that would leave me, again, decades after that meeting, puzzled. On 14th October 1935 she wrote to her nephew Julian in China: "I must now go and see an importunate and unfortunate Gerwoman who thinks I can help her with facts about Women under Democracy – little she knows – what you do about your poor old Virginia." I was shocked. Me? Born in Brooklyn. Importunate? Unfortunate? Gerwoman? As if I were some refugee, washed up on British shores.

The next day, Woolf complained in her diary the she "couldn't write this morning; & must go up & receive Miss Grueber (to discuss a book on women & fascism – a pure have yer as [her parlor maid] Lotte would say)." "A pure have yer"—what did it mean?

Though hurt by her diaries (she was nasty even to some of her best friends), I remembered a compliment she had unwittingly paid me all those years ago, when I sent her my book. "I try to avoid reading about my writing when I am actually writing," she claimed. "I find that it makes me self-conscious and for some reason distracts me from my work." She added that she had loaned my book to "a friend, who is an excellent critic," who told her I had written "a most sympathetic and acute study" of her books. Vita Sackville-West's son, Nigel Nicolson, informed me that the "excellent critic" was Woolf herself. He diffused the diary entry by explaining that "a pure have yer" was slang: "It suggests a throw-away attitude, cockney bravado, suggesting a task forced upon one which needs to be done." He wrote one of my friends, "I was glad to read in VW's diary that she was quite flattered by what Dr. G wrote about her which was rare for Virginia." And he added in a letter to me, "It's one of the things I deplore about Virginia, her cattiness, contempt for almost everyone who were not her friends, an occasional touch of anti-Semitism, her snobbishness and jealousy. But it's almost heresy to suggest these things to the Virginia Woolf Society of the USA."

In 2004, three letters from Virginia turned up in the back of a filing cabinet. Each one had arrived while I was abroad; my mother had tucked them away for safekeeping and then had forgotten to give them to me. On June 21, 1935, Woolf thanked me "sincerely for having taken this interest in my work. That in itself is a great encouragement to me. And I need not say that I hope it will have a success with the public." On October 12 she answered my request to interview her for my book which she believed to be about women and fascism. "I should of course be glad to do anything I can to help you in your work; and will arrange to see you if possible. But as I am not a politician and have no special knowledge of the subject on which you are writing I fear that it would probably be only a waste of your time to see me." In January 1936, she typed a letter to me herself – there are eighteen corrections – in which she expressed her agony in writing *The Years*, a book of frustrations. She confided, "The last stages are always the most dreary until my mind is free from this drudgery."

These three letters, along with the two beautiful ones Leonard found after she committed suicide, helped me deal with my anger and disillusionment. My feelings now seem trifling in comparison to the agony she suffered. Her correspondence with me helped restore the admiration I had for her when I was 20, reveling in her genius, her integrity, and her will to create as a woman.

ABOUT THE AUTHORS

DEIRDRE BAIR is the author of four biographies, whose subjects include Simone de Beauvoir, Anaïs Nin, C. G. Jung, and Samuel Beckett (National Book Award), and a cultural history of late-life divorce. She was a university professor of comparative literature, writes and reviews frequently for many publications, and is currently writing a biography of the artist/cartoonist, Saul Steinberg.

WILLIAM BEEKMAN has been reading and collecting Woolf for almost forty years.

RACHEL COHEN is the author of *A Chance Meeting: Intertwined Lives of American Writers and Artists*. Her essays have appeared in *Best American Essays*, the *New Yorker*, the *Guardian*, and the *New York Times*. She teaches at Sarah Lawrence College.

SARAH FUNKE has overseen three previous publications related to Woolf and her circle for Glenn Horowitz Bookseller, Inc., and countless others on a range of topics in 20th-century literature.

RUTH GRUBER wrote the first doctoral thesis in English on Virginia Woolf, as a 20-year-old American exchange student at the University of Cologne. In 1936, with Hitler in power, the Tauchnitz Press in Leipzig published her thesis, after which Woolf invited her to tea at 52 Tavistock Square. In 1944 as a member of the Roosevelt administration, she secretly escorted 1,000 refugees from Italy to the US. Her book *Haven* telling that story was made into a CBS mini-series. Among her other 19 books are *Witness*, *Exodus 1947*, *Raquela* and *Virginia Woolf: The Will to Create as a Woman*.

MARK HUSSEY is Professor of English at Pace University in New York, where he edits *Woolf Studies Annual*. Among his works on Woolf are *Virginia Woolf A to Z* and *Virginia Woolf and War*.

ANDREW SOLOMON is the author of National Book Award winning *The Noonday Demon: An Atlas of Depression*, and other works of non-fiction and fiction. He is a regular contributor to the *New Yorker* and the *New York Times*.

PETER STANSKY is the Frances and Charles Field Professor of History Emeritus at Stanford University. Among other works he is author of *On or about December 1910: Early Bloomsbury and its Intimate World* and co-author of *Journey to the Frontier: Julian Bell and John Cornford*.

ELIZABETH HARTLEY WINTHROP is the author of novels *Fireworks* and *December*.

NOTES

1 Quoted in Lee 146
2 Lee 68
3 To Dorothy Brett, March 5, 1923
4 July 19?, 1926
5 *Diary* November 15, 1921
6 *Diary* August 16, 1922
7 *Diary* October 4, 1922
8 *Diary* November 3, 1918
9 February 25, 1916
10 "My Early Beliefs," quoted in Rosenbaum 52
11 Dall'Agnol 155-163
12 Quoted in Rosenbaum 21
13 Levy 276
14 August 25, 1916
15 September 30, 1916
16 August 3, 1908
17 Quoted in Dall' Agnol 155-163
18 Quoted in Quentin Bell v. 1, 205-06
19 *Moments of Being*, "Old Bloomsbury," 167
20 *Diary* March 8, 1918
21 Hussey 116
22 October 15, 1931
23 October 1931, quoted in *Letters IV* 391
24 March 21, 1924
25 Schell, 326-335
26 March 1912
27 To Violet Dickinson, Madge Vaughan, Janet Case, Ottoline Morrell, May-June 1912
28 June 1912
29 Schell 326-335
30 Bazin 75 quoted in Hussey
31 To Violet Dickinson, September 21, 1909
32 Clive Bell 64 quoted in Spalding, 119
33 Vanessa Bell, "Memoir VI: Professor Quentin Bell," quoted in Spalding 119
34 Quentin Bell, *Bloomsbury Recalled* (Columbia University Press, 1995), 51-52
35 Roger Fry, *Cézanne: A Study of His Development* (The Noonday Press, 1958), v
36 Virginia Woolf, *Roger Fry* (The Hogarth Press, 1940), 151-52
37 Spalding, 125
38 Woolf, 153
39 Ibid.
40 Ibid., 159
41 Ibid., 155
42 Spalding, *Vanessa Bell*, 105
43 Roger Fry, *Vision & Design* (Penguin Books, 1937), 233
44 All quotations this paragraph, Woolf 180
45 Woolf 286
46 Lehmann 27
47 Rhein 16-17
48 "Pablo Picasso," *International Dictionary of Ballet*, 2 vols., St. James Press, 1993
49 July 30, 1925
50 May 22, 1917
51 Ibid.
52 *Diary* November 25, 1921
53 Rhein 23
54 Rhein 24
55 *Diary* July 28, 1923
56 Willis, 300 quoted in Hussey, 117
57 *Diary*, November 18, 1924
58 *Diary*, January 29, 1939
59 *Diary*, December 2, 1939
60 Quoted in Hussey, 118
61 *Diary*, April 10, 1932
62 *Diary* November 15, 1918
63 *Diary* September 28, 1921
64 October 17, 1940
65 June 23, 1922
66 *Diary* August 16, 1922
67 December 1924, *Dial*
68 Rhein 15
69 January 12, 1923
70 March 5, 1923
71 October 15, 1928

72 Lyndall Gordon, *Virginia Woolf: A Writer's Life*, 1984, 75

73 Quoted in Isaac 14

74 *Diary* June 1923

75 *Diary* mid-October 1923

76 Bell v.1, 60-61

77 December 8, 1917

78 quoted in Hussey 168

79 May 14, 1925

80 From "The Art of Biography"

81 *Diary*, August 21, 1935

82 Quentin Bell, *Virginia Woolf*. New York: Harcourt Brace Jovanovich, 1972, 182

83 *Diary*, July 19, 1938

84 *Diary* June 23, 1929

85 April 17, 1926, *Nation and Athenaeum*

86 May 31, 1938

87 May 11, 1926

88 "A Week in France with Virginia Woolf," in *Virginia Woolf: Interviews and Recollections,* edited by J. H. Stape. Iowa City: University of Iowa Press, 1995, 34

89 September 27, 1928

90 October 5, 1928. Pater's essay on Vézelay was published in *The Nineteenth Century* in June 1894 and reprinted in his *Miscellaneous Studies: A Series of Essays* (1895). He describes there the "great narthex" and the "nave of ten bays, the grandest Romanesque interior in France, perhaps in the world."

91 September 5, 1926

92 July 8?, 1927

93 October 14, 1927

94 September 8, 1928

95 "Moments of Being: 'Slater's Pins Have No Points'." *A Haunted House*. London: Hogarth Press, 1943, 93

96 *The Complete Shorter Fiction of Virginia Woolf*, edited by Susan Dick, 2nd ed. San Diego: Harcourt Brace, 1989, 220

97 For enlightenment on this mystery, see Janet Winston, "Reading Influences: Homoeroticism and Mentoring in Katherine Mansfield's 'Carnation' and Virginia Woolf's 'Moments of Being: "Slater's Pins Have No Points"'" in *Virginia Woolf: Lesbian Readings*, edited by Eileen Barrett and Patricia Cramer. New York: New York University Press, 1997, 57-77. Winston traces the lineage of the carnation as signifier of homosexuality to that worn by Oscar Wilde.

98 *A Haunted House,* 91

99 "A Week in France ," 35

100 August 19, 1930

101 "A Week in France ," 36

102 June 24, 1933, 378

103 "A Week in France," 35

104 September 28, 1928

105 *A Room of One's Own*, 1929. *Orlando*: Harcourt, 2005, 41

106 "The Landscape of a Mind," *Encounter* 2 (January 1954), 70-72, 74

107 *The Waves*, 1931. New York: Harcourt Brace Jovanovich, 1959, 143

108 November 23, 1926

109 Hussey 363

110 Buchan

111 Marcus, quoted in Hussey 260

112 June 5, 1938

113 Hussey, 259

114 February 21, 1930

115 Banks, quoted in Hussey

116 June 16, 1930, and August 1930

117 Woolf, memoir of Julian, in S.P. Rosenbaum, ed. *Virginia Woolf: The Platform of Time: Memoirs of Family and Friends,* London: Hesperus Press, 2007.

118 Hussey 98

119 July 28, 1923

120 July 1, 1926

121 February 12, 1927

122 February 11, 1932

123 November 21, 1934

124 January 29, 1937

BIBLIOGRAPHY

Annan, Noel Gilroy. *Leslie Stephen: His Thought and Character in Relation to His Time.* Cambridge, Mass.: Harvard University Press, 1952.

———. *Leslie Stephen: The Godless Victorian.* New York: Random House, 1984.

Bell, Clive. *Old Friends.* London: Chatto & Windus, 1956.

Bell, Quentin. *Bloomsbury.* New York: Basic Books, 1968.

———. *Virginia Woolf.* In two volumes. London: The Hogarth Press, 1972.

Connolly, Cyril. *The Modern Movement.* New York: Atheneum, 1966.

Dall' Agnol, Darlei. *Dictionary of Literary Biography, Volume 262: British Philosophers, 1800-2000.* A Bruccoli Clark Layman Book. Edited by Philip B. Dematteis, Peter S. Fosl, and Leemon B. McHenry. The Gale Group, 2002.

Hussey, Mark. *Virginia Woolf A-Z.* New York: Oxford University Press, 1995.

Isaac, Alan. *Virginia Woolf, The Uncommon Bookbinder.* London: Cecil Woolf, 2000.

King, James. *Virginia Woolf.* New York: W.W. Norton, 1995.

Kirkpatrick, B. J. *A Bibliography of Virginia Woolf,* 3rd ed. Oxford: Clarendon Press, 1980.

Lee, Hermione. *Virginia Woolf.* London: Chatto & Windus, 1996.

Lehmann, John. *Thrown to the Woolfs: Leonard & Virginia Woolf and The Hogarth Press.* New York: Holt, Rinehart & Winston, 1979.

Levy, Paul. *G.E. Moore and the Cambridge Apostles.* London: Oxford University Press, 1981.

Luedeking, Leila and Michael Edmonds. *Leonard Woolf: A Bibliography.* Winchester/New Castle, Del.: St. Paul's Bibliographies/Oak Knoll Books, 1992.

Palmer, Alan, and Veronica Palmer. *Who's Who in Bloomsbury.* Brighton: The Harvester Press, 1987.

Rhein, Donna E. *The Handprinted Books of Leonard and Virginia Woolf at The Hogarth Press, 1917-1932.* Ann Arbor, Mich.: UMI Research Press, 1985.

Rosenbaum, S.P. *The Bloomsbury Group.* Toronto: University of Toronto Press, 1975.

Schell, R. D. "Leonard Woolf," *Dictionary of Literary Biography, Volume 100: Modern British Essayists, Second Series.* A Bruccoli Clark Layman Book. Edited by Robert Beum. The Gale Group, 1990.

Spalding, Frances. *Roger Fry: Art and Life.* Black Dog Books, 1999.

Spotts, Frederic, ed. *Letters of Leonard Woolf.* New York: Harcourt, Brace, Jovanovich, 1989.

Washington State University. *Catalogue of Books from The Library of Leonard and Virginia Woolf.* Brighton: Holleyman & Treacher Ltd., 1975.

Willis, J. H., Jr. *Leonard and Virginia Woolf as Publishers: The Hogarth Press, 1917-41.* Charlottesville and London: University Press of Virginia, 1992.

Woolf, Leonard and Trekkie Ritchie Parsons. *Love Letters: Leonard Woolf and Trekkie Ritchie Parsons (1941-1968).* Edited by Judith Adamson. London: Chatto and Windus, 2001.

Woolf, Leonard. *Downhill All the Way.* New York: Harcourt, Brace & World, 1967.

———. *Beginning Again.* London: The Hogarth Press, 1965.

Woolf, Virginia. *The Diary of Virginia Woolf.* Five volumes. Edited by Anne Olivier Bell. Assisted by Andrew McNeillie. New York: Harcourt, Brace, Jovanovich, 1978-1984.

———. *The Essays of Virginia Woolf.* Four volumes. Edited by Andrew McNeillie. London: The Hogarth Press, 1986.

———. *The Letters of Virginia Woolf.* Six volumes. Edited by Nigel Nicolson. Assisted by Joanne Trautmann. London: The Hogarth Press, 1975-1980.

Woolmer, J. Howard. *A Checklist of The Hogarth Press 1917-1946.* Revere, Pa.: Woolmer/Brotherson Ltd., 1986.

One thousand copies printed. Set in Rilke and Kelly Sans types.

Printed on Mohawk paper by Capital Offset.

Designed by Jerry Kelly.